Current Perspectives in Psychology

Patient Adherence to Medical Treatment Regimens

Bridging the Gap Between
Behavioral Science and Biomedicine

Alan J. Christensen

YALE UNIVERSITY PRESS   NEW HAVEN AND LONDON

Set in Adobe Garamond, Gill Sans and Torino Modern type
by The Composing Room of Michigan, Inc.
Printed in the United States of America.

ISBN: 0-300-10349-2

Library of Congress Control Number: 2004041522

A catalogue record for this book is available from the British Library.

The paper in this book meets the guidelines for permanence
and durability of the Committee on Production Guidelines for
Book Longevity of the Council on Library Resources.

10 9 8 7 6 5 4 3 2 1

To Gary B. Mertlich, 09/04/54−7/17/02

Contents

Series Foreword

Current Perspectives in Psychology presents the latest discoveries and developments across the spectrum of the pyschological and behavioral sciences. The series explores such important topics as learning, intelligence, trauma, stress, brain development and behavior, anxiety, interpersonal relationships, education, child-rearing, divorce and marital discord, and child, adolescent, and adult development. Each book focuses on critical advances in research, theory, methods, and applications and is designed to be accessible and informative to nonspecialists and specialists alike.

Patient adherence to medical treatment procedures is a critical issue facing physicians today. A surprisingly large proportion of patients do not fill or refill prescriptions, take their medicine, or continue to take it for the recommended treatment period. Even individuals with life-threatening conditions may not adhere to treatment.

Patient Adherence to Medical Treatment Regimens is of broad relevance to the health, medical, and behavioral sciences. Advances in treatment, particularly the development of medications, are ongoing with the implication that the identification of effective treatments is the major obstacle to improving mortality and morbidity. In fact, many effective treatments are already available. A neglected obstacle is the critical stage of getting patients to use the treatments and to follow instructions on which effectiveness depends. This topic is relevant to everyone. Much of the focus of medicine and health care is on prevention of disease and disability. Recommendations for diet, exercise, substance use (e.g., alcohol and cigarettes), vaccinations, and health check-ups, if followed, would have enormous impact on the personal, social, and economic burden of disease. The challenge is how to foster such adherence to treatment regimens.

Alan Christensen discusses the severity and scope of this problem of nonadherence, going well beyond reviewing and lamenting the scope of the problem. He covers theory and research on the nature of the problem, factors that influence adherence, and needed changes in health care delivery. Many factors contribute to whether and the extent to which patients follow through with treatment, including the patient's personality characteristics, the availability of social support in the patient's environment, the context in which treatment is provided, and characteristics of the health care provider. For example, how physicians interact with patients contributes to how well patients adhere. Christensen elaborates how the many factors can be integrated to understand and to improve patient adherence. He makes recommendations in relation to clinical care, research priorities, and health policy.

The book covers a central issue in health care that is relevant to both physical and mental health. The book sheds new light on the problem by proposing new ways to conceptualize the problem and to intervene. We are fortunate to have the benefit of Christensen's deep understanding of the scope of the problem and his recommendations for what changes might be made to improve health. His scholarly and clinically relevant contributions to this area of research have contributed enormously to understanding the interface of patient care and service delivery. The significance of the book derives from the authoritative statement he provides and from the fact that much can be done to improve health.

Alan E. Kazdin
Series Editor

Preface

The desire to take medicine is one feature which distinguishes man, the animal, from his fellow creatures.

Sir William Osler, 1894

As a behavioral scientist and clinical health psychologist, I have devoted a substantial part of my professional life over the past fifteen years to studying the issue of patient adherence to medical treatment regimens. This often-cited quote by Sir William Osler, one of the pre-eminent figures in the history of medicine, has long been a favorite of mine but has also increasingly struck me as incomplete. I say this because of the now well-established fact that patients' apparent unwillingness or inability to take medication as prescribed, or to adhere to medical treatment regimens more generally, reflects a pervasive barrier to effective and safe health care delivery. As those of us who work in medical contexts or with medically treated patients are keenly aware, patient nonadherence is ubiquitous in nearly all clinical populations and exists in all corners of the health care system. This maladaptive pattern of behavior poses a severe toll in terms of increased treatment failures, greater patient morbidity and mortality, and substantial societal and economic burden that has few equals in contemporary health care.

This book reflects an effort to broadly examine the issue of patient adherence with medical treatment regimens. The perspective that I adopted in writing the book stresses the inherently behavioral nature of health care delivery while at the same time underscoring the need for better integration of behavioral science into biomedical research and practice. An underlying theme of the book is that within behavioral science theory, research, and practice, there exists a substantial, largely untapped potential for addressing the problem of patient nonadherence in medical treatment contexts. In each chapter of the book I attempt to delineate this potential in a way that will prove interesting to both behavioral and biomedical scientists, useful to health care practitioners actively addressing these issues "in the trenches" of health care delivery, informative to health care policy makers, and accessible to interested nonexperts including health care consumers and the many other potential readers who are affected by this issue at some level.

Although this book is not intended to provide an exhaustive review of the large scientific and clinical literatures on patient adherence, the central issues that underlie these literatures and that appear to have the greatest potential for shaping future adherence research, practice, and policy, are addressed in turn. In chapter 1, the scope of the nonadherence problem is described, the burden of this "epidemic" is illustrated, and the fundamental but essential issue of developing and applying valid and reliable methodologies to assess adherence is addressed. The second chapter examines the role of behavioral science theory in understanding what is, after all, a fundamentally behavioral phenomenon. This chapter will argue that our understanding of patient adherence can be greatly facilitated by applying broad fundamental theorizing about psychological and behavioral processes and behavior changes that have, to this point, seldom been applied to the phenomenon of patient adherence behavior. Chapter 3 provides a systematic and detailed summary and integration of the many published studies devoted to identifying determinants of patient nonadherence. Characteristics of the treatment regimen itself, patient sociodemographic characteristics, patient psychological characteristics, social support and social environment factors, and provider characteristics are all examined. Chapter 4 is largely devoted to presenting a particular theoretical perspective (the *person X context interactive perspective*) and supporting evidence that I believe will be useful in helping to reconcile the inconsistent and admittedly disappointing data that have accumulated concerning determinants of patient adherence and are useful in helping to shape future research questions and methodologies.

Chapters 5 and 6 are both devoted to the critical issue of designing and evaluating interventions to facilitate patient adherence behavior. Chapter 5 reviews the broad array of intervention approaches that have been the subject of attention from adherence researchers and summarizes what is known about the efficacy of the various strategies. Chapter 6 examines some of the key conceptual and methodological issues that adherence intervention researchers must tackle in order to progress further in this vital area of research. Finally, in Chapter 7, I discuss some of the ways in which critical transdisciplinary efforts at addressing the adherence issue might be fostered. To be successful, a shift in perspective is required of both behavioral scientists and practitioners, and medical practitioners. The time is right for behavioral scientists to apply their unique talents, resources, and perspectives to this important clinical problem that to date has received surprisingly little attention from this group. This type of application holds the most promise for effectively addressing what is truly a behavioral epidemic.

Acknowledgments

Series editor Alan Kazdin provided an important early stimulus for this book and allowed me to contribute to what is shaping up to be an outstanding series, "Current Perspectives in Psychology." Erin Carter, the behavioral and social sciences editor at Yale University Press, was always available to provide me much-needed assistance as the book became a reality. In my ten years at the University of Iowa I have had the good fortune of working with a series of outstanding graduate student assistants. Jamie Johnson and Katherine Raichle are two of the best and I extend my thanks to both of them for assistance with this project. Most important, it is my extreme good fortune to have a wonderful wife and son who always elevate my spirits and give me an incentive to do my best no matter what the crisis or how far the temperature falls. Thank you, Deb and Aaron.

1

The Challenge of Patient Adherence

Implications and Assessment

The dawn of the twenty-first century may be the most exciting period in the history of modern health care. Each year brings another remarkable increase in biomedical knowledge. Each passing day seems to bring news of a new and potentially groundbreaking medical technology that carries a new source of potential healing for patients in need. From the potential of a human genome map to facilitate the detection, prevention, and treatment of disease in future generations, to the promise of a fully implantable artificial heart for prolonging the lives of tens of thousands of individuals each year, the potential ability of medicine to prevent, diagnose, and treat disorders is poised for heights unimaginable only three decades ago.

As exciting as the science of modern medicine has become, the practice of health care and medicine continues to be impeded by an age-old Achilles' heel. The potential effectiveness of biomedicine's advances continues to rely on the willingness and ability of human beings to change their behavior. Systematic behavior change is required at nearly every stage of the medical treatment process and for virtually every type of health-related intervention (see figure 1.1). Whether med-

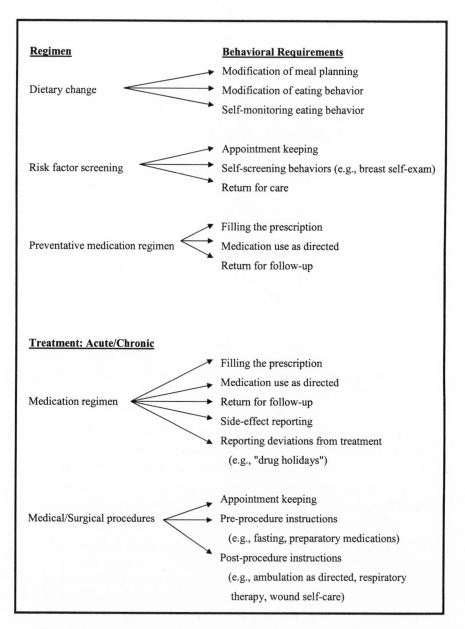

Fig. 1.1. Common behavioral requirements for effective medical treatment delivery.

ical intervention requires a patient to follow a prescribed medication regimen, involves making a dietary or other lifestyle change, or simply requires an individual to attend a clinic appointment or a prescribed procedure, patient behavior change (that is, *patient compliance or adherence*) is, in virtually all cases, a necessary condition for safe, effective, and cost-efficient health care delivery. It is, unfortunately, a condition that often goes unmet.

Defining the Problem

Slightly different definitions of the terms *patient compliance* and *patient adherence* have been offered over the years in the behavioral and health science literatures (e.g., DiMatteo & DiNicola, 1982; Feinstein, 1990; Liptak, 1996; Turk & Meichenbaum, 1991). Some previous authors have suggested that the term *compliance* reflects an overly authoritarian view of health care that unduly minimizes the patient's role as a decision-maker and that the alternative term, *patient adherence,* offers a more collaborative view of provider–patient exchanges (Eisenthal et al., 1979). The term adherence is generally used in the behavioral science literature and is increasingly seen in the allied health science (e.g., nursing, psychology, pharmacy) literatures. However, the term patient compliance is still common parlance in the medical literature (e.g., Feinstein, 1990). I use the terms interchangeably at times, but the term patient adherence will generally be used throughout this book, as it is most consistent with both the recent, broader literature and an underlying theme of this volume: that maximizing the success of health-related assessments and interventions requires explicit provider–patient collaboration.

Although previous definitions of patient adherence/compliance have varied somewhat in the literature, they have comprised a generally consistent set of core elements. Definitions have emphasized the expert opinion or direction of the health care provider offered with the goal of preventing or treating disease, along with the extent to which patient behavior mirrors that direction. With these elements in mind I suggest the following working definition: *patient adherence reflects the extent to which a person's actions or behavior coincides with advice or instruction from a health care provider intended to prevent, monitor, or ameliorate a disorder.*

The Achilles' Heel of Modern Health Care

Although estimates of patient nonadherence have varied widely across
adherence measures, regimens, settings, and populations, the available
data suggest that between 20 and 80 percent of patients do not adhere
to the basic requirements of their medical treatment regimen (Dunbar-
Jacob & Schlenk, 2001; Sackett & Snow, 1979; Turk & Meichenbaum,
1991). High rates of nonadherence have been consistently documented
for both minor and severe medical problems, for both genders, and
across all ages, ethnic groups, and socioeconomic strata. Based on my
own descriptive review of the adherence literature including the illustrative studies described below, and keeping in mind the substantial
between-study variability in nonadherence estimates, the rate of nonadherence appears to be highest for preventive regimens or treatment
of asymptomatic patients, slightly lower for chronic regimens in symptomatic populations, and "lowest" for time-limited regimens in acutely
ill patients (see table 1.1). It is important to note that "lowest" in this
case is a relative term, as patient nonadherence seems nearly epidemic
across all treatment regimen categories. Studies of pharmacotherapy
records have indicated that approximately 20 percent of all medication
prescriptions written by a physician are never even filled by the patient
(Burns et al., 1992; Boyd et al., 1974). Even among patients who are
otherwise cooperative in following a medication schedule, approximately 20 percent are believed to take "drug holidays" (several consec-
utive days without medication) each month (Urquhart & Chevalley,
1988). Stated simply, patient nonadherence is the Achilles' heel that
modern health care has simply been unable to shake.

Preventive regimens. Some unique patterns of adherence behavior
have been identified for certain treatment regimen categories. Studies

Table 1.1 Most frequently reported rates of nonadherence by regimen type.

Regimen type	Rate of nonadherence
Preventive regimens	50–80%
Chronic treatment regimens	30–60%
Acute treatment regimens	20–40%

of medications specifically prescribed for preventive reasons suggest particularly poor adherence. This is not surprising given that preventive regimens, by definition, are directed toward reducing the risk of a less salient, potential disorder or problem in patients who may be free of any current symptoms. For example, less than one-third of patients at risk for infection following dental procedures comply with the prescribed antibiotic guidelines even though a regimen as brief as one to two doses of medication is often used (van der Meer et al., 1992; Blinder et al., 2001). Similarly, more than two-thirds of postmenopausal women discontinue prescribed estrogen-replacement therapy within two years of starting (Kayser, Ettinger, Pressman, 2001). Low rates of adherence to preventive regimens appear to extend to parental behavior (Liptak, 1996). For example, a recent study reported that only 27 percent of parents of iron-deficient infants purchased the iron supplementation that had been recommended for their child (Amsel et al., 2002). Other preventive measures meet with similarly poor adherence. Approximately half of individuals adopting an exercise program quit within six months (Dubbert, 1992), and 50 to 60 percent of individuals fail to keep clinic appointments related to preventive care (DiMatteo & DiNicola, 1982).

Chronic treatment regimens. The failure of patients to comply with chronic treatment regimens is nearly as common as for preventive interventions. Adherence is poor among most chronically ill populations despite the fact that the consequences of nonadherence are typically more salient for these patients. Studies involving patients receiving life-sustaining renal dialysis have typically observed that between 30 and 60 percent of dialysis patients do not adhere to diet, fluid-intake, or medication regimens (Christensen & Ehlers, 2002). These numbers are particularly alarming given that nonadherence in this population has been linked to a variety of medical complications and greater mortality risk (Wolcott et al., 1986; Kimmel et al., 2000). Patients receiving treatment for hypertension are believed to exhibit particularly poor rates of adherence with between 40 and 60 percent of individuals failing to take their antihypertensive medications as instructed (Clark, 1991; Lee et al., 1996; Mallion et al., 1998). In one study involving patients with long-standing, serious hypertension, 61 percent failed to take their antihypertensive medications as prescribed

(Lee et al., 1996). Data suggest that more than half of patients infected with tuberculosis are nonadherent with antituberculosis drug treatment (Al-Hajjaj & Al-Khatim, 2000). Adherence is similarly poor among patients receiving medication to treat established coronary artery disease (e.g., Straka et al., 1997).

Troubling rates of patient nonadherence have been reported even when the potential consequences of not following a treatment protocol are severe. For example, in a recent study of women with stage I and II breast cancer, nearly two-thirds failed to complete the entire prescribed course of radiation therapy (Li et al., 2000). Growing evidence suggests that treatment adherence among HIV-infected individuals is particularly troubling. Adherence to the new, potentially quite effective, "highly active antiretroviral therapy" (HAART) drug combinations has proven to be particularly problematic (Cinti, 2000). Despite the substantial and widely disseminated evidence that these medications can greatly reduce viral levels and forestall the onset of AIDS, recent data indicate that approximately half of patients receiving the medications fail to take the drugs as prescribed (Nieuwkerk et al., 2001).

Pediatric treatment regimens. As vexing as the problem of nonadherence in adult populations has proved to be, research suggests that nonadherence is even more common among pediatric populations. Problematic adherence among children and adolescents is not surprising given the unique challenges inherent in this population (see review by Liptak, 1996). Treatment-related information is typically communicated to a parent or caregiver who has responsibility for the minor child's care rather than to the patient him- or herself, increasing the possibility of errors in communication or understanding. The physical development of young children may be limited in ways that make treatment administration more difficult (e.g., inability to swallow pills). Moreover, until ages six to seven the child's stage of cognitive development limits his or her ability to understand the need for medical care and the comprehension of somewhat abstract treatment-related cause-and-effect relationships (e.g., unpleasant medication leading to improvement in symptoms or painful injections forestalling future illness).

One frequently cited study estimated that only 5 percent of parents adhered to the antibiotic regimen prescribed for their child's middle ear infection (Mattar, Markello, & Yaffe, 1975). Another early study reported that fewer than 20 percent of children receiving penicillin by mouth for the treatment of potentially serious streptococcal infection received the medication for the required ten-day treatment course (Bergman & Werner, 1963). More recent data paint a similarly alarming picture. In one study, prescription refill records indicated that only 12 percent of infants and young (less than five years old) children at risk for pneumonia due to sickle cell disease received oral antibiotics according to the schedule prescribed by their pediatricians (Elliott et al., 2001). Moreover, the primary cause of penicillin treatment failure in streptococcal tonsillitis in children is now believed to be lack of compliance with the ten-day treatment regimen (Pichichero et al., 2000).

The rate of nonadherence among children receiving chronic treatment regimens is similarly bleak. Studies of asthmatic children have generally found that more than half of the children fail to use inhaled asthma medications as prescribed (Milgrom et al., 1996; Sherman, Baumstein, Hendeles, 2001). From 40 to 50 percent of children and young adults with diabetes fail to have glucose levels monitored adequately, do not have important dietary modifications instituted, and fail to receive oral medication or insulin injections as prescribed (Altobelli et al., 2000; Thompson et al., 1995). Adherence rates are poor throughout childhood with the worsening adherence generally observed during the adolescent years when children presumably begin to manage their diabetic regimen more independently (Bond, Aiken, Sommerville, 1992). This lack of adherence to various aspects of the diabetic regimen clearly undermines blood glucose control. In a study of 268 children and adolescents with diabetes, only one-third achieved the recommended degree of blood glucose control (i.e., HbA1c level < 8%) (Thomsett et al., 1999). These high rates of nonadherence in childhood, and the poor diabetic control that results, coincide with substantially greater risk of visual impairment, kidney disease, vascular disease, and other diabetic complications in later life (DCCT, 1993).

As adolescence progresses, children have the potential to take on more responsibility for their own treatment-related decisions and actions, but this developmental period is also characterized by a sense of invulnerability, increasing antagonism toward authority figures, risk-taking behavior, and lack of a future-oriented time perspective. Each of these developmental characteristics poses a potential barrier to adherent patient behavior. Accordingly, adolescence is known to be a time of particularly problematic treatment delivery (e.g., Bond et al., 1992).

Lack of provider recognition. Despite tremendous scientific evidence, volumes of text discussion, and countless anecdotal examples that many, if not most, patients fail to follow prescribed treatment regimens, health care providers appear to have little awareness of nonadherence among their own patients. Most commonly, providers greatly overestimate the extent to which their own patients comply with treatment recommendations (Bangsberg et al., 2001; Goldberg, Cohen, & Rubin, 1998; Norell, 1981). For example, in a study of patients being treated for gastric ulcer, physicians overestimated patient medication intake by nearly 50 percent (Roth & Caron, 1978). Similar results were obtained in a more recent study involving forty-five HIV positive individuals being treated with antiretroviral medications (Bangsberg et al., 2001). In this study, physicians correctly identified only 40 percent of the nonadherent patients. While inadequate physician awareness of adherence is a problem across all medical specialties and all levels of physician experience, less experienced providers appear to have the most difficulty identifying patient nonadherence. Brody (1980) reported that 79 percent of "easily detectable" medication noncompliance went unrecognized by interns and residents in internal medicine. This lack of recognition of nonadherence and the corresponding inability of health care providers to make appropriate adjustments in a treatment regimen certainly magnifies the potential harm that patient nonadherence poses to the individual and to the public health (e.g., Rudd, 1993).

The Burden of a Behavioral Epidemic

The numbers themselves are striking. Inadequate patient adherence is a pervasive problem and it is one that carries a profound personal, societal, and economic cost. As many as 10 percent of all hospital admissions are believed due to nonadherent patient behavior (Col, Fanale, Kronholm, 1990). While nonadherence-associated costs for specific patient groups differ widely, they are nearly universally high (see review by Cleemput, Kesteloot, & DeGeest, 2002). For example, among patients being treated with antihypertensive medication, nonadherence to the medication regimen has been associated with more than

$800 per patient year in increased hospitalization and other health care costs (McCombs, Nichol, Newman, & Scalr, 1994). For more involved or expensive medical interventions the economic impact of nonadherence rises accordingly. Noncompliance among renal transplant patients, for example, has been estimated to result in an additional $9,000 per patient year in hospitalization costs alone (Swanson et al., 1992).

Estimates of the total economic costs of medication nonadherence across all patient groups are depicted in table 1.2. These costs include $25 billion annually in additional medical treatment expenses, $5 billion in additional nursing home admissions, and a total of more than $100 billion a year when lost productivity and total economic impact is considered (Berg et al., 1993). Because these estimates involve only medication nonadherence, they likely underestimate the cost implications of nonadherence to all health care regimens. When considered relative to other behavioral or psychological problems, the tremendous economic burden of patient nonadherence has few equals. Total medical costs attributed to smoking are approximately $50 billion (CDC, 1994). The total economic impact of drug abuse and dependence, including lost worker productivity, has been estimated at $98 billion (NIDA, 1992).

The economic costs are staggering but, of course, tell only a small part of the story. Overall estimates of premature death or increased disease are difficult to come by, and there is obvious variability between conditions and treatments. In virtually all clinical populations in

Table 1.2. Annual economic costs of noncompliance.

Source of costs	$ billion
Revenues from unfilled new and refill prescriptions	8
Hospital admissions linked to noncompliance	25
Nursing home admissions linked to noncompliance	5
Lost productivity caused by noncompliance	>50
Premature deaths caused by noncompliance	?
Health costs in ambulatory patients linked to noncompliance	?
Total costs	100 plus

Source: Berg et al., 1993.

which the issue has been addressed, however, patient nonadherence to treatment has been definitively linked with treatment failures, illness relapse and complications, increased disability, and in many cases premature death. For example, in organ transplant patients, failure to adhere to lifelong immunosuppressant drug treatment leads to organ rejection (Rovelli et al., 1989). As many as 75 percent of renal graft rejection episodes resulting in kidney failure in the second year after transplant may be due to nonadherence (Kiley, Lam, & Pollak, 1993). In renal dialysis patients, failure to adhere can lead to serious bone disease, hypertension, congestive heart failure, and earlier mortality (Christensen & Ehlers, 2002). Individuals with diabetes who fail to tightly control blood sugar levels through adherence to glucose monitoring, dietary, insulin use, and medication regimens are known to be at a significantly elevated risk for a myriad of complications of the disease and shortened survival (DCCT, 1993). One recent report suggests that failure to adhere to antihypertensive medication regimens may be the single biggest contributor to this medicine's inability to control serious high blood pressure (Stephenson, 1999). As many as half of failures of treatment to control blood pressure are believed due to patient nonadherence that goes unrecognized by the provider (Stephenson, 1999). In addition to an increased risk of medical complications (e.g., stroke, kidney disease, cardiovascular disease) due to hypertension, this pattern of nonadherence results in unwarranted increases in medication dose and unnecessary changes to more potent, sometimes more dangerous, medication.

It is also becoming increasingly clear that nonadherence to certain medications may undermine the efficacy of the treatment for future use in other individuals. An increasing concern in the treatment of HIV/AIDS is the recognition that a lack of patient adherence to antiretroviral regimens is resulting in virus mutations that are increasingly resistant to drug therapy (Kelly & Kalichman, 2002). Similar public health concerns have arisen in regard to various bacterial infections. Many antibiotics are becoming less effective at fighting such common bacteria as streptococcus and tuberculin due to antibiotic resistance due, in large part, to a failure of patients to follow and complete antibiotic treatments as prescribed (Leclercq, 2001).

Implications for medication testing and treatment guidelines. The impact of nonadherence on future treatment effectiveness likely occurs in a variety of ways. It is becoming increasingly recognized in the pharmacology literature that patient nonadherence poses a serious barrier to medication testing and trials and to the development of valid, empirically based treatment guidelines for medication usage (Urquhart & Chevalley, 1988). As Urquhart and Chevalley (1988) have discussed, medication nonadherence certainly occurs in drug trials just as it occurs in nonresearch treatment contexts. Nonadherence in the drug trial phase poses a very troublesome problem, as establishing a safe and effective therapeutic dosing range for a medication is particularly difficult when an unknown but substantial number of clinical trial participants are missing an unknown number of medication doses. To date, pharmaceutical researchers have not had an adequate answer to this problem. One strategy for devising medication guidelines in light of poor medication adherence has been to set the recommended and prescribed dosing range high enough so that a therapeutic level of the medication is maintained even for patients who miss a substantial number of missed doses (Urquhart & Chevalley, 1988). This strategy, however, may pose a risk of iatrogenic overdosing effects in patients who actually do comply with these "adjusted" dosing guidelines.

One intriguing suggestion from the pharmacology literature has been to stratify the reported efficacy of a given medication according to various degrees of patient adherence (Urquhart & Chevalley, 1988). If adherence is explicitly assessed in medication trials, the differential efficacy of the medication across different levels of adherence could be determined and reported. This strategy is intriguing because it could provide practitioners and patients the potential for making a more informed, empirically based, and collaborative decision about how a medication regimen might be tailored for a particular patient (that is, based on the presumed level of patient adherence). For this approach to be successful, however, adherence must be accurately assessed, a vexing issue that we turn to in the next section. Moreover, providers must have the ability to predict, at the time of treatment implementation, which patients are likely to be nonadherent to treatment, a difficult prerequisite indeed and one that I address in the following chapter.

The Assessment of Adherence

From an assessment perspective, patient adherence has proven to be an extremely elusive phenomenon to capture. Adherence is a behavioral process, but direct behavioral measures of the process (for example, actual observation of regimen-related behavior) are generally impractical and are seldom used. Clearly, no gold standard exists for adherence assessment in most patient populations or treatment regimens. The widely ranging estimates of nonadherence reported in the research literature and the lack of insight many health care providers have about nonadherence in their own patients are likely to both be due, at least in part, to a lack of practical, reliable, and valid adherence measurement tools.

Subjective adherence reports. Five general categories of adherence measures are available to the researcher and the practitioner (see table 1.3). Subjective patient self-report remains the most widely utilized assessment strategy despite fairly consistent evidence that self-reports may substantially underestimate actual nonadherence rates (e.g., Epstein & Clauss, 1982; Spector et al., 1986; Waterhouse et al., 1993). As discussed earlier, subjective physician appraisals of patient adherence are known to be similarly inaccurate (e.g., Bangsberg et al., 2001; Goldberg, Cohen, & Rubin, 1998; Norell, 1981).

Patient self-reports of adherence are inexpensive and can be efficiently gathered with little or no technical expertise, but they are inherently limited. Patients may be reluctant to disclose nonadherent behavior to the health care provider that prescribed the treatment. Even patients who are well intentioned are likely to have difficulty accurately recalling adherence to a sometimes complicated treatment regimen. Recall of behavioral events in general is known to be fallible and subject to a variety of memory biases (see Stone & Shiffman, 2002). As Dunbar-Jacob and Schlenk (2001) have discussed, patients tend to be most adherent at or near the time of a clinic visit or when they anticipate their adherence is to be evaluated. When providers ask patients to recall their adherence behavior over a longer, past time period, the patients' recollections may be biased by their most recent (and typically most adherent) behavior. Stone and colleagues (2000) have discussed the advantages of utilizing repeated, discrete, momentary self-assessments of behavior. Momentary assessments are likely to minimize re-

Table 1.3. Adherence assessment methods.

Measurement category	Examples of assessment methods
Subjective reports	Patient self-report (retrospective or momentary assessment) Caregiver/informant reports Health care provider estimates
Biological/Biochemical indicators	Blood levels of medication or of medication metabolites Medication tracers (e.g., Phenobarbital) Blood/serum levels of targeted substances (e.g., blood glucose levels in diabetes; serum phosphate levels in renal dialysis) Physical markers (e.g., intersession fluid weight gains in hemodialysis)
Indirect measurements	Pill counts Prescription refill records Electronic medication monitoring
Direct measurement	Appointment keeping Treatment refusal or treatment "shortening" Physical activity sensors Medical device monitoring
Clinical/Health outcomes	Hospitalization frequency Blood pressure changes Disease severity Treatment outcome (e.g., infection resolution; organ rejection)

call biases because they ask patients to report on a particular behavior in "real time" throughout the day rather than relying on patient "reconstruction" of adherence behavior over several days or weeks. This approach appears highly promising but is itself imperfect. The limitations of this approach involve a much greater time demand on the patients' part when asked to record or report data on a frequent basis and the related problem of potentially poor adherence to the self-assessment protocol itself.

Biological and biochemical indicators of adherence. A second gen-

eral type of adherence assessment involves reliance on indirect biological or biochemical indicators of patient behavior. Measures of this type
are generally free from memory lapses or reporting biases, but they are
usually imperfect reflections of actual patient behavior and should be
considered cautiously. The usefulness and the validity of this measurement approach varies greatly across patient populations and treatment
regimens. For example, for individuals with insulin-dependent diabetes this approach has proved to be fairly useful. For these patients,
blood glucose control depends significantly (although not entirely)
upon adherence to the diabetic self-treatment regimen (for example,
frequency of insulin injection, frequency of blood glucose testing, dietary behavior) (Cox & Gonder-Frederick, 1992). Self-reports of adherence to specific aspects of the regimen may be questionable, and repeated assessments of blood-glucose levels are difficult to obtain, but a
widely available blood test of glycosylated hemoglobin (HbA1) level
provides a reliable and valid indication of mean blood glucose regulation over an approximately eight-week period (Blanc et al., 1981).
HbA1 levels are routinely used for clinical purposes and are the most
widely used measure of diabetic control in the adherence research literature (Cox & Gonder-Frederick, 1992).

Adherence studies involving hemodialysis patients often examine biochemical markers as measures of adherence behavior. Some of
these are quite suspect. For example, serum potassium (K) levels are
sometimes examined as an indication of whether a patient has been
following the necessary low potassium diet. However, serum K levels
are known to be influenced by changes in the dialysis treatment itself,
by some medications, and by a variety of acute medical conditions. In
contrast, adherence to the fluid-intake restrictions required of hemodialysis patients can be accurately determined by simply comput-
ing the amount of weight a patient gains between dialysis treatment
sessions (Manley & Sweeney, 1986).

A related strategy sometimes used to assess medication adherence
is to attempt to monitor the blood or serum level of the medication (or
a metabolite of the medication) itself. As a gross indicator of whether a
medication has been taken at all, this strategy generally works well
(Roth, 1987). The problem arises when more specific information is required, like the amount of medication that has been taken or when it

was taken. Blood levels of many medications are known to be influenced by a variety of factors other than patient behavior (Roth, 1987). For example, in organ-transplant patients, blood levels of the most common immunosuppressive medications (e.g., cyclosporine, tacrolimus) are unstable over time and are influenced by a number of factors (e.g., individual differences in metabolism rates, food intake, other medications, acute illness) other than treatment adherence (Christensen & Ehlers, 2002). Some researchers have suggested that "spiking" a medication with a marker or tracer compound (low doses of phenobarbital is most commonly used) may be an effective approach to adherence assessment (Feely et al., 1987; Roth, 1987). Examinations of the reliability of the tracer compounds themselves suggest significant pharmacokinetic variation in tracer levels, however, making these levels less than perfect proxies for actual medication adherence (Pullar et al., 1988; Shine & McDonald, 1999).

Indirect adherence assessments. A third general strategy involves the use of such indirect methods as pill counts, medication monitors, or prescription refill rates to ascertain patient adherence. Considerable evidence suggests that pill counts are an insensitive indicator of medication adherence (Roth, 1987). In a study of ninety-one individuals with serious hypertension followed over a three- to five-month period, pill counts showed little concordance with other methods of assessing medication adherence (Lee et al., 1996). In this study, only 37 percent of patients identified as nonadherent based on presumably more reliable electronic monitoring of medication usage were classified as nonadherent based on pill counts. Similarly, a study of 179 individuals being treated for Type 2 diabetes found that pill counts failed to identify 87 percent of the patients deemed to be nonadherent based on biochemical assessment (Pullar et al., 1988).

Adherence researchers have increasingly turned their attention toward electronic monitoring of medication dosing. Unlike pill counts, the newest generation of electronic monitors allows for some determination of whether the medication was taken in the manner prescribed (i.e., at the correct time of day or at the correct dosing interval). The most commonly used electronic medication-monitoring technology is the MEMS (Medication Event Monitoring System, Cramer et al., 1989). The MEMS has been used to assess adherence in

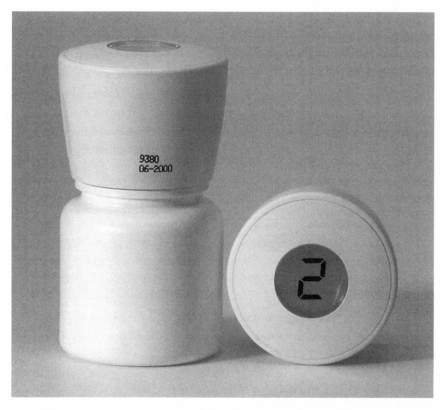

Fig. 1.2. MEMS electronic medication dose monitor. From AARDEX Ltd., 2002.

nearly three hundred clinical trials and other research protocols (APREX, 1998). The MEMS "TrackCap" (see figure 1.2) records the date and hour each time the medication bottle cap is removed. Each cap opening is treated as a presumptive medication dose. Data are automatically stored for up to eighteen months in a small microprocessor fitted to each bottle cap. This information is then downloaded to a computer so that health care providers or researchers can see patterns of medication taking.

Considerable data suggest that electronic monitoring provides a more sensitive measure of nonadherence to medication regimens than do simple pill counts or many other measurement strategies (Farmer,

1999). For example, in a study of adherence during an antihypertensive medication trial, pill counts suggested near perfect patient compliance. Electronic monitoring, however, revealed that fewer than half of all cap openings occurred during the prescribed twelve-hour interval (± 2 hours) (Rudd et al., 1990). In a study of patients taking antiepileptic medication, pill counts suggested adherence rates between 90 and 99 percent depending on dosing interval, and electronic monitoring revealed that patients were adherent as few as 39 percent of the days evaluated (Cramer et al., 1989). Electronic monitoring clearly is superior to simple pill counts as an adherence assessment methodology, but it is much more expensive and still imperfect. As with simple pill counts, the amount of medication a patient has removed from a MEMS cap or other dispenser relies on the assumption that medication removal is synonymous with medication ingestion. The accuracy of this assumption has yet to be adequately evaluated.

Pharmacy or prescription refill records reflect another possible indicator of medication adherence. Pharmacy records may approximate the quantity of medication used, and they appear to be more accurate than some other methods. Some evidence suggests that pharmacy records provide a more valid and reliable indicator of medication adherence than do patient self-reports (Frick et al., 1998) or physician estimates (Sherman et al., 2000). They are clearly imperfect, however, and also appear to overestimate adherence (Paes, Bakker, & Soe-Agnie, 1998). In a study of adherence to medication treatment for peptic ulcer disease, the correlation between the amount of medication obtained (determined through pharmacy records) and a presumably reliable urine test for the presence of the medication was only .47, indicating only modest agreement between the two sources of information (Roth, 1987). As previous authors have discussed, a central limitation of pharmacy records as an adherence measure is that they say little or nothing about the timing or consistency of medication doses, an important consideration for most medications (e.g., Choo et al., 1999; Paes, Bakker, & Soe-Agnie, 1998).

Direct measurement of adherence. Some studies have utilized more *direct measures* of adherence-related behaviors. Appointment keeping is the most common example of this strategy (e.g., Hershberger, Robertson, Markert, 1999; Mirotznik et al., 1998). A patient's presence at a scheduled appointment can be determined with near certainty. A patient may miss an appointment for a variety of reasons, however, some of which are clearly under a patient's direct behavioral control, while other reasons may not be. Moreover, empirical evidence has indicated that the association between appointment keeping and other adherence indices (e.g., medication adherence) is modest at best (Roth, 1987).

Electronic monitoring tools have been used in the assessment of adherence in several populations. In research involving adherence to physical activity recommendations, electronic motion sensors have proved useful (Schlenk et al., 2000). Accelerometers can, for example, provide a reliable estimation of energy expenditure throughout the day by incorporating acceleration and deceleration information as well as distance traveled (Dunbar-Jacob, Schlenk, & Caruthers, 2002). In the renal dialysis population, an electronic device designed to record the degree to which a patient's prescribed home peritoneal dialysis schedule is being followed has recently been introduced (Diaz-Buxo et al., 1999). This "memory card" is inserted into a specially adapted dialysis machine prior to use and stores a range of parameters related to the dialysis process over a two-month period. Among asthmatic patients, electronic monitoring of inhaler use over multiple weeks of usage appears to be a promising methodology (Bender et al., 2000). With these few exceptions, strategies for the direct assessment of adherence behavior have not proved particularly useful.

Clinical changes and health outcomes. Finally, some studies have utilized clinical changes (e.g., blood pressure changes) or health outcomes (e.g., hospitalization frequency) as proxies for patient adherence (Binstock & Franklin, 1988; Dickinson et al., 1981). As reviewed earlier, empirical data support the presumption that clinical outcomes are correlated with adherence in virtually all treatment populations. Utilizing clinical or health outcomes as proxies for patient adherence presents at least two problems, however. First, poorer physical health is itself predictive of less adherent patient behavior (Sherbourne et al., 1992). A decrease in health status may have preceded a decline in adherence, making cause-and-effect interpretations difficult or impossible to determine. Second, the extent of the correlation between adherence and heath outcomes varies widely and is, in many cases, not well known.

On balance, my recommendation is that clinical changes or health outcomes be treated as important outcomes in their own right that may be partially mediated by adherence behavior, but are not synonymous with or adequate proxies for gauging actual regimen adherence.

In Conclusion

Patient nonadherence to medical treatment regimens is pervasive, costly, difficult to measure, and despite its significance often goes unrecognized or unmeasured by practitioners. Because it impedes the healing potential of virtually all modern medical advances, nonadherent patient behavior may be the single most important challenge faced by health care practitioners today. A fundamental step toward addressing this challenge is to enhance the assessment and ultimately the recognition of patient nonadherence. All of the currently available adherence measures and assessment methodologies are limited in one or more important ways. Some methodologies are unreliable or are difficult to interpret, some are impractical or expensive, and many measures are subject to systematic biases in recall, judgment, or social desirability. Given these limitations, it is critical for researchers and practitioners alike to utilize multiple indicators of patient adherence to minimize the impact of the limitations or idiosyncrasies of a single methodology.

Recent evidence suggests that lack of treatment adherence not only is harmful to the nonadherent patient him- or herself but may also undermine the efficacy of some treatments for future patients. As such it is truly a public health problem of epidemic proportion. As a behavioral phenomenon it is also a problem that behavioral science is uniquely qualified to address. Just how successful behavioral science has been in this regard, how it might be more successful in the future, and how the dominant perspective in contemporary health care must be realigned to facilitate this success are some of the central issues to be addressed in this volume.

2

The Role of Behavioral Science Theory in Patient Adherence Research

What is the role of behavioral science theory in understanding what is, fundamentally, a behavioral phenomenon? Surprisingly, perhaps, the role of such theory in understanding adherence behavior has thus far been a very limited one. There have been few attempts to articulate a cohesive and empirically testable set of behavioral or psychological principles that seek to explain what factors influence adherence behavior or how adherence might be facilitated. In some cases, researchers and past authors have attempted, with limited success, to apply more general theories about human behavior to the issue of patient adherence with little attempt to tailor the theory to fit the unique aspects of the adherence process. This is the case for several of the cognitive-social psychological models to be reviewed in this chapter. In other cases, theorists have offered compelling arguments for the relevance of a particular model or framework, but the argument has garnered little or no empirical attention. Several of these broader behavioral models are potentially relevant to furthering our understanding of patient adherence but have not been adequately tested in this context. In this and the following chapter, I examine the utility of several models from the broader social psychology, personality psychology, and clinical psychology literatures that have previously received little consideration from adherence researchers but which can usefully inform our thinking about patient adherence.

The Health Belief Model

The role of patient beliefs or cognitions in influencing health-related behavior has held a prominent place in health behavior theory and research for over three decades. A number of related models and constructs have been applied to the prediction of health behavior in general, and treatment adherence specifically, and are discussed in this chapter. The single most influential model in this regard has been the *Health Belief Model* (HBM; Rosenstock, 1966). Initially developed to explain individual differences in preventive health behavior (Hochbaum, 1958), the HBM was later applied to adherence to both acute and chronic medical treatments (Becker & Maiman, 1975). The HBM can be construed as a subjective-expected-utility or "expectancy-value" decision-making model (see Janis, 1984). That is, the fundamental presupposition of the HBM is that individuals are rational decision makers who select a course of action after systematically evaluating and comparing the values and probabilities associated with each possible alternative.

More specifically, according to the HBM (see figure 2.1), individuals are most likely to adopt a particular behavior when a perceived health threat is high and when the perceived health benefits of the behavior in question outweigh any barriers. Perceived threat is a function of how susceptible an individual perceives he or she is to a given possible negative health outcome and how severe that potential outcome is perceived to be. Perceived benefit generally refers to the extent to which the individual believes that adopting the behavior in question will avert the negative health outcome (although other potential benefits might also be considered). Perceived barriers to adherence are construed broadly in the model and include both tangible barriers (e.g., monetary cost of the treatment; time investment required) and more

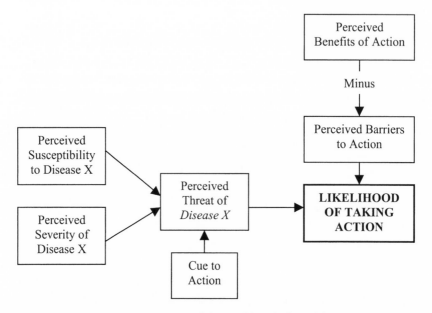

Fig. 2.1. Diagram of the Health Belief Model.

subjective or socioemotional barriers (e.g., concern over side effects; social stigma associated with the regimen). In one formulation of the model, a "cue to action" (e.g., receiving information about a health threat, experiencing symptoms related to a health threat) is implicated as an important precursor to trigger or maintain a health behavior change (Strecher, Champion, & Rosenstock, 1997). The importance of this aspect of the HBM has received little attention.

Although the HBM has enormous intuitive appeal, the utility of the model in predicting health behavior in general and treatment adherence specifically has proved to be modest. Perhaps not surprising given the origins of the model, research involving the HBM and preventive health behavior is the most compelling (e.g., Stein et al., 1992; Cummings, Jette, & Brock, 1984; Ronis, 1992). For example, among women over the age of thirty-five, perceived barriers to practicing breast self-examination (e.g., lack of time, embarrassment) were associated with less frequent examinations, and perceived susceptibility to breast cancer was associated with more frequent practice (Champion, 1990). Similar results have been obtained for mammography screening

(Stein et al., 1992), safe-sex practices (Basen-Engquist, 1992), cigarette smoking (Strecher et al., 1997), immunization behavior (Cummings, Jette, & Brock, 1984), preventive dental care (Barker, 1994), and a variety of other preventive health practices. However, the data are not entirely consistent. Some studies involving components of the HBM and preventive health practices have failed to find the predicted associations (e.g., Alagna & Ready, 1984; Montgomery et al., 1989). For example, in a report involving HBM predictors of AIDS-preventive behaviors, Montgomery and colleagues reported no association between perceived susceptibility, barriers, or benefits, and risky sexual behavior over an eighteen-month follow-up period.

On balance, the data involving aspects of the HBM and preventive health practices suggest a modest but fairly consistent association between these health beliefs and behavior. Evidence regarding the utility of the HBM in the prediction of medical regimen adherence among patients with existing disease is more limited than is the case for preventive behaviors (Strecher et al., 1997). Although not entirely consistent, studies involving a range of illness and treatment groups (e.g., hemodialysis, organ transplantation, diabetes, hypertension) have demonstrated that patients reporting greater perceived barriers to following a treatment regimen (e.g., being away from home for treatment or follow-up, medication costs, medication side effects) show less favorable adherence than do other patients (Horne & Weinman, 1999; Glasgow, McCaul & Schaefer, 1986; Richardson, Simons-Morton, & Annegers, 1993; Kiley et al., 1993). For example, in a study involving sixty-five individuals with insulin-dependent diabetes, perceived barriers to following the diabetic control regimen predicted adherence to various aspects of the regimen including regularity of blood glucose testing, exercise frequency, and adherence to the insulin injection guidelines (Glasgow et al., 1986). Reported barriers to adherence included embarrassment or perceived social stigma, the time commitment required, and the technical difficulty of insulin administration.

The relation of the other components of the HBM (e.g., perceived threat, perceived benefits of adhering) to adherence is inconsistent and much less clear (e.g., Fincham & Wertheimer, 1985; Rosenbaum & Ben-Ari Smira, 1986; Taylor, 1979; Wiebe & Christensen, 1997). In a study examining dietary, fluid-intake, and medication adherence among seventy patients receiving hemodialysis, none of the HBM components were directly associated with any adherence measure (Wiebe & Christensen, 1997). Rosenbaum & Ben-Ari Smira (1986) concluded that a failure of the HBM to predict adherence more consistently among some chronic illness groups was due to the difficulty inherent in executing and maintaining the required behavioral changes even among well-intended patients. From this perspective, models like the HBM are likely to be more successful at predicting or explaining behavioral intentions or self-reported motivation to adhere, and somewhat less successful at predicting actual behavioral adherence to a regimen that may be demanding or requires certain behavioral or self-control skills the patient may not adequately possess (e.g., the ability to delay gratification).

Irrational Health Beliefs

Janis (1984) argued that a major limitation of the HBM and other expectancy-value models (e.g., Theory of Reasoned Action; Protection Motivation Theory; both to be discussed later in this chapter) involves the assumption that health-relevant information is appraised and acted upon in a rational manner. As Janis has described, health-related decisions are often conflicted, based on somewhat ambiguous information, and are themselves stressful to make. Under these conditions, Janis has argued, it is difficult for individuals to make "high-quality" adaptive or rational decisions. From this perspective, when an individual is prone to appraising a situation in a distorted manner, conventional definitions of "rational" health beliefs (such as is presumed by the HBM) are not as likely to predict health behavior.

Consistent with Janis's perspective, Christensen, Moran, & Wiebe (1999) have proposed that irrational health beliefs or health-related cognitive distortions may play a more central role in determining nonadherent behavior than do more conventional conceptualizations of "rational" health-related cognitions or beliefs. In our work and interactions with nonadherent patients, my colleagues and I have long made the anecdotal observation that nonadherent patients often engage in seemingly systematic errors in information appraisal. One of the first medically ill patients I evaluated as a psychology intern was a college-educated sixty-five-year-old woman with a history of difficult-to-control hypertension. In discussing with her a recent appointment with her physician I asked what instructions her physician had given her about her blood pressure medications. She replied, "Well, he wants me to take a new medicine, but I'm not going to do it." I asked why she was not planning to follow her physician's instruction. To this she replied, "Because my sister tried this same medicine a few years ago and it did not help her a bit." It was difficult for this well-educated and intelligent woman to separate her own experience from that of another individual, at another time, with a different medical history.

Such patients seem to hold relatively rigid cognitive templates for viewing and interpreting health-related experiences in ways that are at times inconsistent with any objective evidence or even with some commonly accepted view of reality. This style of information appraisal is reminiscent of the systematic and enduring information-processing biases or cognitive errors that have been described among individuals prone to depression (Alloy & Abramson, 1988; Beck, 1967). For example, as was the case with one of my early patients, some individuals are prone to making overgeneralizations about health-related experiences on the basis of an irrelevant past experience (e.g., "This medication did not help my friend's condition, therefore it is not useful for me"). Other individuals may be prone to making irrational inferences about common but unpleasant treatment-related effects (e.g., "A medication that makes me feel tired can't be good for me to take"). These errors often seem to belie additional patient education or attempted instruction or clarification on the part of the health care provider.

To test the relevance of this type of irrational appraisal to adherence, Christensen, Moran, & Wiebe (1999) developed the twenty-item Irrational Health Belief (IHBS) scale to assess individual differences in the tendency of patients to engage in health- or treatment-related cognitive distortion or irrational appraisals. In a study of 107 Type 1 diabetic patients, we found that higher IHBS scores (reflecting greater cognitive distortion) were associated with significantly poorer self-reported adherence to the multifaceted diabetic regimen as well as poorer blood glucose control (Christensen, Moran, & Wiebe 1999). These results suggest that more conventional, rationalistic views of the cognitive underpinnings of patient adherence may be insufficient as

they do not consider the possibility that well-intended efforts to inform patients about their health might be subject to distortion or
misappraisal. Further research involving the IHBS measure and the
broader construct of health-related cognitive distortion certainly is
necessary before firm conclusions can be drawn about the importance
or unique relevance of this construct relative to more conventional
conceptualizations of patient health beliefs.

Theory of Reasoned Action and Theory of Planned Behavior

The *Theory of Reasoned Action* (TRA) was developed as a more general
(non-health-specific) theory of volitional human behavior (Ajzen &
Fishbein, 1980). The TRA (see figure 2.2) rests on the assumption that
behavioral intentions are strong predictors of behavior change and that
these intentions are primarily influenced by the attitudes an individual
holds toward the behavior and by perceived social norms. Attitudes,
from the TRA perspective, include the expected consequences (both
positive and negative) an individual holds about a behavior and the
value or importance of those consequences. Perceived social norms re-
fer to beliefs an individual holds about what others expect or desire of
him or her in regard to a particular behavior (i.e., "what do others want
me to do"). The value or importance the individual places on how others will react to a behavioral decision (i.e., "do I care what others
think") is also deemed important. The desires or expectancies of those
closest or most salient to an individual ("significant others") are given
the greatest credence in the model. It is the social norm component
that most distinguishes the TRA from the Health Belief Model and
other attitudinal or expectancy-based models of health-related behavior.

As applied to health-related behaviors, the model predicts that an
individual will adopt a particular behavioral response (e.g., regimen
adherence) when the expected consequences of the behavior are relatively favorable (e.g., a health threat is reduced), the expected consequences are important (e.g., the health threat reduction is valued), and
the behavior is consistent with perceived social norms (e.g., significant
others prefer that the individual adopts the behavior). The *Theory of*

Planned Behavior (TPB) (see figure 2.3) is a slightly reformulated version of the TRA in which an individual's perceived degree of control over a target behavior (termed *perceived behavioral control*) is considered in addition to the social norm and attitudinal components of the earlier model (Ajzen, 1988). As is the case for the Health Belief Model, the TRA and TPB presume that individuals engage in a rationalistic weighing of the evidence before coming to a decision.

Research involving the TRA has generally supported the utility of the theory and the importance of attitudes and perceived social norms as predictors of behavioral intentions and, to a lesser extent, actual behavior (Madden, Ellen, & Ajzen, 1992; Shepard, Hartwick, & Warshaw, 1988). The majority of this research, however, has involved non-health-related behavior (e.g., purchasing decisions; investment choices; voting behavior). Although health behavior applications of the TRA are less common than for other behaviors, the available evidence clearly supports the importance of the various components of the model to the prediction of preventive health behaviors (Maddux & DuCharme, 1997). Studies involving exercise behavior (e.g., Norman & Smith, 1995), safer-sex practices (Reincke, Schmidt, & Ajzen, 1996), dietary behavior (e.g., Oygard & Rise, 1996), alcohol use (O'Callaghan et al., 1997), health screening (e.g., Sheeran, Conner, & Norman, 2001), and weight reduction (Schifter & Ajzen, 1985) have all suggested that attitudes or beliefs one holds about the consequences of a behavior, along with perceived social norms regarding the behavior, explain a significant amount of variability in the behaviors themselves.

The incremental value of the perceived behavioral control component that distinguishes the Theory of Planned Behavior (TPB) is not entirely clear. A review of the literature involving these models and exercise behavior concluded that perceived behavioral control has generally failed to predict significant variance in behavior beyond that accounted for by attitudes and social norms (Godin, 1993). However, a more recent review that did not distinguish health-related from non-health-related behaviors concluded that perceived behavioral control is indeed predictive of behavior over and above the attitudinal and social norm components (Armitage & Conner, 2001). Madden, Ellen, & Ajzen (1992) have further argued that the relevance of perceived control as a predictor of behavior within the TPB increases as the actual

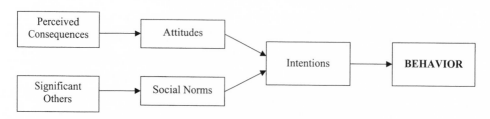

Fig. 2.2. Diagram of the Theory of Reasoned Action.

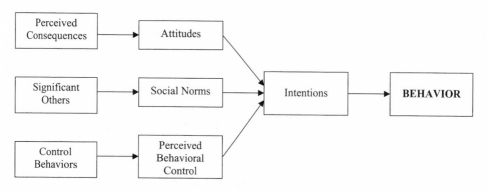

Fig. 2.3. Diagram of the Theory of Planned Behavior.

controllability of the target behavior decreases. In this study by Madden and colleagues, higher perceived behavioral control was a better predictor of actual behavior for relatively low control behaviors (e.g., "getting a good night's sleep") than for relative high-control behaviors (e.g., "renting a videocassette"). Few health-related behaviors were considered in this study, however.

Perhaps not surprisingly, in the case of TRA and TPB research, studies have almost universally found that the models are better predictors of behavioral intentions than of the actual target behavior. Some studies have failed to even include an actual behavioral indicator. Moreover, many studies that have reported a significant association between attitudes, normative beliefs, perceived behavioral control, and "behavior" have relied on potentially suspect self-reports of behavior with no collateral or objective behavioral measure. A comprehensive review of the statistical effects reported in 185 TPB studies found that the overall model (i.e., attitudes, social norms, perceived behavioral control) was strongly predictive of behavioral intentions and self-reports of behavior, and somewhat less strongly (but still significant statistically) predictive of actual (objectively defined) behavior (Armitage & Conner, 2001).

Although data involving the association of the TRA or TPB models and preventive health practices are encouraging, research involving the models and regimen adherence in individuals with established disease is scant. There is some evidence that patient attitudes toward the treatment are associated with adherence to time-limited antibiotic regimens (Reid & Christensen, 1988), adherence to the lithium regimen among individuals with bipolar affective disorder (Cochran & Gitlin, 1988), and to the extent to which parents are adherent to medication the giving guidelines prescribed for their children with epilepsy (Austin, 1989). However, there are far too few studies examining the Theories of Reasoned Action or Planned Behavior to draw any conclusions about the potential relevance of these models to the management of existing disease.

In sum, the Theory of Reasoned Action extends the Health Belief Model in its premise that perceived social norms play an important role in influencing behavioral decisions. The Theory of Planned Behavior reflects a further extension of earlier models in its consideration of perceived behavioral control as an important determinant of behavior. As is the case for the Health Belief Model, the TRA and TPB can be construed as subjective-expected utility models that presume an individual comes to a decision about a potential course of behavior after rationally weighing the expected costs and consequences. Although the available evidence consistently demonstrates an association between the tenets of the models and preventive health practices, many studies have been marked by such important methodological limitations as a common reliance on potentially biased self-reports of health behavior and a tendency for some studies to equate behavioral intentions with actual behavior. Little evidence exists concerning the relation of either model to acute or chronic medical treatment regimens. It is simply not known if the seemingly positive findings for health practices are generalizable to other forms of adherence behavior. Finally, the evidence concerning the role of perceived behavioral control in predicting health behavior or adherence is inconsistent. One interpretation of this inconsistency is that individual differences in perceived control are most important for behaviors that are more challenging or more difficult actually to exert control over. From this perspective, the perceived behavioral control aspect of the model will likely prove more important for highly complex or behaviorally demanding medical regimens (e.g., the diabetic control regimen) and less meaningful for understanding less complex target behaviors (e.g., exercise behavior).

Protection Motivation Theory

An additional expectancy-value model that has had an enduring impact on the way we think about health behavior change is the *Protection Motivation Theory* (PMT; Rogers, 1975, 1983). The PMT was developed to explain how "fear appeals" influence an individual's attitudes toward a target (usually health-related) behavior. Fear appeals reflect attempts to persuade or motivate an individual to change an attitude or behavior by providing information that the behavior poses a threat. The PMT is composed of three fundamental components (see figure 2.4). First, two sources of information, environmental and intrapersonal, are presumed to initiate cognitive processing concerning a potential threat. Environmental sources include receiving information about a threat and observing others' experiences with a threat. Intrapersonal sources of information include an individual's prior experiences and personality differences. Once information is received, cognitive processing about the threat ensues. This processing centers on two types of appraisals: appraisals about one's vulnerability to the threat and the severity of the threat if nothing is done (considered a "maladaptive response" by the model), and appraisals of one's ability to cope with and avert the consequences of the threat through a behavior change (considered an "adaptive response"). As with the other expectancy-value models (e.g., the Health Belief Model), PMT specifies a weighing of the costs and benefits of a particular behavioral coping response. Specifically, coping appraisals consider efficacy expectancies ("can I change my behavior?") and response expectancies ("if I change my behavior will the threat be reduced") less any anticipated costs associated with the behavioral response.

The degree of "protection motivation" an individual possesses is

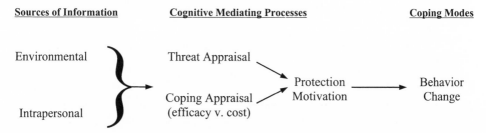

Fig. 2.4. Diagram of Protection Motivation Theory.

a combined function of the threat appraisal and coping appraisal processes. The degree of protection motivation then determines whether
an individual will change behavior or not. That is, under conditions of
high threat, high self-efficacy, and net-positive response expectancies,
an individual should possess a high degree of motivation or intention
to protect oneself and, presumably, to cope with the threat by making
a behavior change. If, on the other hand, threat is low, self-efficacy is
limited, or the individual expects that engaging in the behavior will result in relatively more costs than benefits, protection motivation and
the likelihood of behavior change is low.

Considerable research has examined the various components of
PMT in regard to a range of health-related and non-health-related behavioral variables. A comprehensive, quantitative review by Floyd,
Prentice-Dunn, and Rogers (2000) revealed several interesting patterns. For example, across a variety of disease prevention and health-
promotion domains (e.g., cancer prevention, AIDS prevention, exercise, alcohol consumption) examined in sixty-five studies, increases in
perceived threat severity, perceived threat vulnerability, self-efficacy,
and expected response efficacy were all associated with a significant cu-
mulative effect on both behavioral intentions and actual health behavior. Unfortunately, few if any studies have examined the utility of
the model as a whole, making it difficult to determine whether these
various elements have any sort of synergistic relationship to behavior
(Rogers & Prentice-Dunn, 1997). As was the case for the expectancy
value or health-belief-based models discussed earlier in the chapter, the
magnitude of the effects for behavioral intentions tended to be somewhat larger than for behavior itself. It was also the case that the major-

ity of PMT studies have been limited by a reliance on self-reports of behavior.

As was the case for the Theory of Reasoned Action and Theory of Planned Behavior, few studies have examined the model in regard to treatment regimen adherence in individuals with existing acute or chronic disease. Only four such studies were identified by Floyd and her colleagues in their search of research published over a twenty-four-year period. In these four studies, the coping variables specified by the model (i.e., self-efficacy, response efficacy, response costs) were much more strongly related to adherence than the perceived threat variables (i.e., vulnerability, severity). This pattern seems consistent with evidence discussed earlier in this chapter that perceived behavioral control and self-efficacy may be more important predictors of adherence to relatively demanding or more complex behavioral regimens than are threat-related appraisals.

In sum, Protection Motivation Theory provides a useful conceptual scheme for identifying cognitive or social cognitive variables that mediate health-behavior intentions and, to a lesser degree, actual health behavior. Most of the individual components of the theory have been demonstrated to have important effects on preventive health practices. There have been very few attempts to test theory as a whole and few studies involving the utility of the model in understanding regimen adherence among individuals with existing disease. As an expectancy-value model there is at least an implicit reliance on the assumption that the decision-maker appraises information in a rational, systematic manner. As is the case for other expectancy-value models, this assumption may limit the predictive utility of Protection Motivation Theory under certain circumstances and for some individuals.

Psychological Reactance Theory

Health behavior researchers have been interested in the relation between control-related beliefs and behavior for more than four decades (Wallston & Wallston, 1982). Despite scores of studies devoted to this topic there have been few attempts to articulate or apply a theory that helps to clarify how and why perceived control is an important mediator of health-related behavior. In the remainder of this chapter I will outline why I believe psychological reactance theory (Brehm, 1966; Brehm & Brehm, 1981) may be quite useful in understanding the motivational basis of nonadherence and its relation to perceived control.

The Theory of Psychological Reactance was articulated to explain the motivational state that arises when an individual perceives that his or her behavioral freedom is threatened or restricted. Several general tenets and hypothesized processes are central to reactance theory. First, when an individual perceives that a "free behavior" (a behavior ordinarily under voluntary control) is restricted or threatened with elimination, the individual's desire to engage in that behavior (or for the object of the behavior) increases. For example, research has shown that when an initially less attractive choice or behavioral option is eliminated, that eliminated option becomes significantly more desirable to the individual (the "forbidden fruit" effect) (e.g., Brehm, 1966). Second, when a behavioral option is restricted or threatened with elimination the individual will be motivated ("react") to preserve or reestablish the option by engaging even more intently in the very behavior that has been threatened. This "boomerang effect" suggests that attempts to discourage individuals from engaging in a behavior may, in fact, have the opposite effect. Such a pattern has been reported in a variety of contexts, including the observation that age requirements on underage drinking behavior may actually increase the frequency of such behavior (Engs & Hanson, 1989). Other research suggests that imposing warning labels or restrictions on violent television programming may increase interest in the programming (Bushman & Stack, 1996). An analogous boomerang or reverse effect of behavioral proscription has also been observed for some alcohol- or drug-prevention messages (e.g., Bensley & Wu, 1991). Finally, according to reactance theory, the greater the perceived importance of the threatened freedom (and the greater number of individual freedoms that are threatened), the greater the individual's motivation to reestablish the freedom will be. For example, research has demonstrated that the increases in desire toward a restricted object or behavioral option is greatest when there are relatively few other options or choices available to the individual (Brehm, 1966).

Shelley Taylor (1979) first described how a variety of seemingly arbitrary restrictions of personal freedom or control are largely inherent in the experience of a medical patient. The patient role implies, and typically requires, some loss of behavioral freedom or relinquishing of control to health care providers and to the medical treatment or hospitalization process itself. Patients are routinely asked to relinquish control over many central aspects of day-to-day and longer-term functioning. In the case of outpatient care this might include restrictions on dietary choices, physical activity level, travel plans, work schedules, and social commitments as well as mandates to take medication or subject oneself to any number of uncomfortable or unpleasant medical procedures. In the case of inpatient medical care the range of restriction on behavioral freedoms extends even further. Hospitalized patients are instructed when and what to eat, what clothes they can and cannot wear, when to sleep, what medications to take, when it is permissible to leave their room, who they must share a room with, when to socialize, and when they can return home. In fact, I would argue that the range and centrality of the restrictions of freedom and loss of control that a typical medical patient is subject to has few parallels in all of human experience.

Despite what appears to be a compelling context for the fundamental principles of Reactance Theory to be operating, the theory has received surprisingly little attention in the adherence literature. Rhodewalt and Strube (1985) outlined a variety of ways that medical patients might exhibit reactance to a perceived loss of freedom or control. Reactant patients might attempt to restore a sense of control by engaging in the restricted behavior or refusing to adopt a prescribed behavior. Reactant patients might also exhibit anger toward the identified agent of their threatened freedoms, the health care provider. Research to date has only indirectly examined the relevance of reactance theory to patient nonadherence. Some researchers have turned to reactance theory to explain observed personologic differences in adherence (Rhodewalt and Marcroft, 1988; Christensen et al., 1994). Rhodewalt and Marcroft (1988) demonstrated that Type A–personality individuals (who are presumably more sensitive to restrictions of personal control) with insulin-dependent diabetes exhibit poorer treatment adherence than their non–Type A counterparts. This pattern was interpreted as suggesting that patients exhibiting the Type A behavior pattern reacted with nonadherence in an attempt to regain perceived behavioral control. There was no attempt, however, to assess whether differences in treatment-related perceived control actually mediated or accounted for the nonadherent behavior. There was some evidence that nonadherent Type A's reported more anger toward their illness than did other patients, possibly indicative of greater sensitivity and reactance toward disease or treatment-related restrictions.

Several more recent studies have examined related constructs or psychometric measures presumed to reflect individual differences in the tendency to exhibit psychological reactance (Donnell, Thomas, & Buboltz, 2001; Fogarty & Youngs, 2000; Moore, Sellwood, & Stirling, 2000; Seibel & Dowd, 1999). However, there are limited data concerning the potential association of these presumably trait measures of reactance with patient adherence. Moore et al. (2000) evaluated neuroleptic medication adherence among thirty-nine patients with schizophrenia who had also completed the Hong Psychological Reactance Scale (HPRS; Hong, 1992). The HPRS was designed to reflect individual differences in the tendency to which an individual strongly values behavioral freedom and freedom of choice, and the extent to which the individual is characteristically resistant or reactant to advice and recommendations from others. Findings were mixed. Higher HPRS scores (presumably reflecting a greater tendency toward reactance motivation) were significantly correlated with self-reports of poorer medication adherence during the period shortly after diagnosis but were not associated with adherence reports in the nine-month period surrounding the study itself. In a study involving a mixed sample of medical patients, Fogarty and Youngs (2000) found a significant association between higher scores on a similar measure of "trait reactance" and self-reported adherence. Adherence was not objectively or directly evaluated in this study.

To date there has been no direct or inclusive examination of the principles or processes central to psychological reactance theory in regard to patient adherence behavior. Moreover, what seems to have been missing is an integrated view of how the various tenets of reactance theory might apply to the various stages of the medical treatment and treatment adherence process. To this end, I present a conceptual map linking reactance theory and patient adherence (see figure 2.5). In this model, various aspects of the medical treatment context are presumed to give rise to a perceived restriction in behavioral freedom or control. It is important to note that the perceived loss of freedom or control can occur in response to attempts to persuade an individual to adopt a new behavior or engage in a prescribed action (e.g., adopt a medication regimen) as well as to requests to give up a valued, existing behavior (e.g., restrict one's diet). This perceived loss of control then leads to the affective and motivational state known as reactance. The reactance state in turn results in nonadherent patient behavior as one avenue for reestablishing threatened control.

The proposed model also recognizes the likely possibility that personologic variables exist that moderate the sensitivity of an individual patient to this perceived loss of control or the likelihood that a state of reactance arises in response to this loss of control. This component of the model is particularly important both because not all individuals display nonadherence in response to objectively identical circumstances, and because alternative, quite distinct reactions to a perceived loss of control (such as helplessness or passive acceptance) also appear to be common in some individuals (S. Taylor, 1979). The utility of this model in furthering our understanding of the nonadherence process in general and the specific relevance of reactance theory to nonadherence awaits explicit study of the paths detailed in the model.

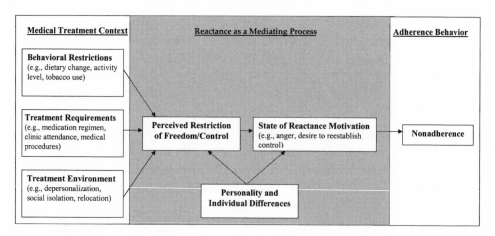

Fig. 2.5. Illustration of Psychological Reactance Theory applied to treatment adherence.

In Conclusion

The application of behavioral science theory to patient adherence behavior has been slow to evolve. Many of the theories that have been applied to the prediction and understanding of health-related behavior reflect similar social learning or social-cognitive principles and constructs. The appraisal of threat or of threat-relevant information is an initiating factor in most theories. Most theories can be construed as expectancy-value models in which behavioral decisions are the result of a systematic consideration of the expected positive and negative consequences of behavior change. Two central assumptions in the expectancy-value models are that behavioral intentions are closely related to actual behavior and that the decision-maker appraises information and evaluates expected outcome in a rational manner free of cognitive biases. Neither of these assumptions appears to have clear empirical support suggesting that a broadening of these theories is in order. Nevertheless, each of these models has played an important role in guiding investigations and helping to shape the literature involving health-related behavior in general, and to a lesser extent, adherence behavior specifically. This chapter closed with an illustration of how one social psychological theory (psychological reactance theory) that has previously received little consideration in the adherence literature might be applied to the phenomenon of treatment nonadherence and may help to clarify the role of perceived control in the adherence process.

Although the theories discussed thus far have had many common elements, they have also generally failed to consider the role of psychological traits or social factors in influencing adherence behavior. The need for conceptual models of adherence that incorporate the role of personologic differences and social factors and processes is clear, and this need is a central focus of the next two chapters.

3

Determinants of
Patient Adherence

Identifying correlates or determinants of patient adherence has been a central goal of adherence researchers for more than four decades. Identifying predictable and consistent determinants of nonadherence is a critical part of understanding why the problem is so prevalent, what patients are at highest risk for nonadherence, and, ultimately, what can be done to ameliorate this costly problem. Despite the fact that hundreds of empirical studies and published articles have been devoted to this goal, our understanding of factors that influence adherence remains modest. In fact, earlier reviews of this vast literature concluded that there is little compelling evidence of an association between any patient individual difference characteristic and treatment adherence (Haynes, 1979; Kaplan & Simon, 1990; Meichenbaum & Turk, 1987). In this chapter I provide a broader and updated critical examination of the literature on adherence determinants and discuss several factors that may have impeded the collective progress of adherence research to date. I examine five broad categories of potential adherence determinants or predictors (see table 3.1), including: *characteristics of the treatment regimen itself, patient sociodemographic characteristics, patient psychological characteristics, social support and social environment factors,* and *provider characteristics.*

Table 3.1. Adherence correlates and predictors from the empirical literature.

Adherence correlates	Representative studies
Treatment regimen characteristics	
Dosing frequency	Girvin et al., 1999; Hamilton & Briceland, 1992
Treatment side effects	Ammassari et al., 2001
Treatment costs	Chisholm et al., 2000; Dodrill et al., 1987
Patient sociodemographic characteristics	
Patient age	Christensen & Smith, 1995; Boyer et al., 1990
Gender	Morduchowicz et al., 1993; Kiley et al., 1993
Socioeconomic status/ Education level	Apter et al., 1998; Lloyd et al., 1993; Sharma et al., 2000
Patient psychological characteristics	
MMPI scores (scales 2,7,0)	Blumenthal et al., 1982; Edinger et al., 1994
Personality traits (neuroticism, conscientiousness)	Christensen & Smith, 1995; Moran et al., 1997
Type A behavior pattern	Cox et al., 1984; Rhodewalt & Marcroft, 1988
Hostility	Christensen et al., 1997b
Locus of control	Brown & Fitzpatrick, 1988; Chen et al, 1999
Self-efficacy	Brady et al., 1997; De Geest et al., 1995; Kavanagh et al., 1993
Patient depression	Carney et al., 1998; Littlefield et al., 1992
Social support & social environment	
Support satisfaction/Support quality	Christensen et al., 1992; Finnegan & Suler, 1985; Catz et al., 2000
Social network size	Kaplan & Hartwell, 1987
Family Environment	Christensen et al., 1992
Parental/familial communication	Davis et al., 1996

Treatment Regimen Characteristics
Regimen Complexity

Examinations of treatment regimen characteristics that may be associated with adherence differences are quite limited, and few consistent findings have emerged. One relatively consistent finding is that less frequent medication dosing (e.g., once per day) is associated with better patient adherence than are more frequent dosing schedules (e.g., three or four times per day) (Girvin, McDermott, & Johnston, 1999; Hamilton & Briceland, 1992; Paes, Baker, & Soe-Agnie, 1997). Not surprisingly, more frequent and more severe treatment side effects are associated with poorer adherence than are treatments with fewer side effects (Ammassari et al., 2001).

More complex or multifaceted treatment regimens are generally believed to result in poorer patient adherence than are simpler regimens (Meichenbaum & Turk, 1987). In the case of the diabetic control regimen, for example, patients are faced with a variety of responsibilities, including the self-monitoring of blood glucose several times per day, the measurement and self-injection of insulin, and monitoring dietary behavior and physical activity levels throughout each day (Cox & Gonder-Frederick, 1992). These responsibilities are in addition to a range of other diabetic self-care activities, including remaining cognizant of physical changes that may signal extreme fluctuations in blood glucose (hypoglycemia or hyperglycemia) and being vigilant about injuries to the hands or feet that might go unnoticed due to a lack of physical sensation in these areas. Given the complexities inherent in the diabetic regimen and the multiple stressors associated with this disease, it is not surprising that nonadherence rates in diabetes are among the highest of any patient population.

Interestingly, research examining adherence to the multiple aspects of the diabetes self-care regimen, as well as adherence in other populations, has observed that the level of adherence to the various aspects of a multifaceted regimen are not highly correlated (Moran, Christensen, & Lawton, 1997; Orne & Binik, 1989). In other words it is common for patients to show poor adherence to some aspects of the treatment regimen while maintaining adequate adherence in other areas. This pattern suggests that in the case of complex treatment regimens "something has to give," and otherwise adherent patients may have difficulty simultaneously managing multiple complex demands.

Treatment Cost

Medication or other treatment cost has been described in some reports as an important barrier to patient adherence (Reichert, Simon, & Halm, 2000). Having to choose between obtaining a prescribed medication refill and purchasing other necessities is certainly not conducive to sustained treatment adherence. Research suggests, however, that the importance of cost as a barrier to adherence is circumscribed. At least one study has found that when otherwise expensive medications are provided to patients free of charge, adherence is somewhat improved over the short term (for the first six months). After this period of time, adherence generally drops off even if medication continues to be offered at no cost (Chisholm et al., 2000). Other evidence has suggested that the amount of out-of-pocket medication costs due to differences in insurance coverage are not associated with significant differences in medication adherence (Dodrill et al., 1987). Although there are certainly economic barriers that limit patient adherence in some cases, even when cost or access to care is not a factor, rates of nonadherence remain high.

Patient Sociodemographic Characteristics

Few consistent patterns involving sociodemographic variables have emerged in the treatment adherence literature (Kaplan & Simon, 1990). The sociodemographic characteristics that have been most consistently associated with differences in adherence are patient age and socioeconomic status. In a number of studies, younger patients have exhibited consistently poorer adherence to treatment regimens across a range of treatment settings and patient populations when compared to older patients (Christensen & Smith, 1995; Boyer et al., 1990; Lloyd et al., 1993; Monane et al., 1996; Thompson et al., 1995). These studies have consistently shown that young adults exhibit better regimen adherence than do adolescents; middle-aged patients show more favorable adherence than younger adults; and older adults may be more adherent to treatment than any other age group. After age sixty-five there is some evidence that adherence begins to decline (Weingarten & Cannon, 1988).

Other evidence has suggested that education level or socioeconomic status is related to treatment adherence. Apter and colleagues (1998) reported that asthmatic patients with less than twelve years of education and lower household income (less than $20,000 annually in this study) exhibited poorer treatment adherence than other patients. Similar findings have been reported among organ transplant patients

(Sharma et al., 2000), coronary artery bypass surgery patients (Harlan et al., 1995), and individuals with Type 1 diabetes (Lloyd et al., 1993). Finally, some evidence suggests that males exhibit significantly poorer adherence than females (Boyer et al., 1990; Morduchowicz et al., 1993; Kiley et al., 1993; De Geest et al., 1995; Lloyd et al., 1993). For example, in a study of 592 adults with insulin-dependent diabetes, women reported significantly better adherence to the diabetes self-care regimen than did men (Lloyd et al., 1993).

Patient Psychological Characteristics

The large majority of studies seeking to identify correlates or predictors of treatment adherence have involved the broadly defined category of patient psychological characteristics (see table 3.1). This chapter focuses on the most common psychological characteristics examined in the adherence literature, including personality traits or dispositions, patient beliefs or expectancies, and patient depression.

Patient Personality

Adherence researchers have long been interested in the possibility that individual differences in personality traits might differentiate adherent from nonadherent individuals. The possibility that personality predictors of adherence exist is intuitively appealing as it is consistent with the premise that personality traits should manifest themselves in terms of consistent patterns of behavior (including health-related or adherence behavior). The idea that trait predictors of adherence exist also has significant potential as a clinical tool. An understanding of relevant personality traits would be useful in the identification of those individuals at greater risk for nonadherence and who may warrant special attention or intervention by health care providers. Although there is clear potential for personality assessment to contribute to our understanding of individual differences in regimen adherence, as the following review will demonstrate, the realization of this potential has often proved difficult.

Standardized personality inventories. Considerable research has examined the utility of using standardized personality inventories as predictors of adherence. The most commonly used inventory in past decades has been the Minnesota Multiphasic Personality Inventory (MMPI; Banks et al., 1996; Blumenthal et al., 1982; Dodrill et al., 1987; Edinger et al., 1994; Mawhinney et al., 1993). The original 566-item MMPI and the more recently revised MMPI-2 were developed by statistically comparing the way that preselected groups of individuals with a variety of psychological disorders or behavioral problems differed from each other and from control groups in their responses to scale items. Results from a number of studies have indicated poorer adherence among individuals scoring higher on MMPI scales reflecting emotional distress (particularly scale 2–depression and scale 7–anxiety) (e.g., Blumenthal et al., 1982; Edinger et al., 1994; Marshall & Roiger, 1996). For example, in a study involving adherence to a prescribed exercise program among thirty-five patients recovering from a myocardial infarction, individuals who failed to complete the program scored higher on MMPI scales reflecting depression, anxiety, and hypochondriasis than did program completers (Blumenthal et al., 1982). Some evidence suggests that patients scoring higher in social introversion (scale 0) (Blumenthal et al., 1982; Kinsman, Dirks, & Dahlem, 1980) and higher in paranoia (scale 6) (Banks et al., 1996) may also show poorer adherence. However, other studies have failed to find few if any associations between MMPI responses and adherence (e.g., Dodrill et al., 1987; Keegan, Dewey, & Lucas, 1987; Mawhinney et al., 1993). In a sample of 282 epileptic patients, Dodrill et al. (1987) reported that the MMPI profiles of adherent and nonadherent groups were essentially identical. In general, few of the associations between MMPI patterns and adherence have been successfully replicated.

Other standardized personality measures have received much less attention in the literature. The Millon Behavioral Health Inventory was specifically designed to assess personologic differences among medical patients with a number of scales believed to be relevant to how a patient responds or adapts to physical illness and its treatment (MBHI; Everly & Newman, 1997; Millon, Green, & Meagher, 1982). Despite the MBHI's conceptual relevance to patient adherence issues, there is scant evidence that the MBHI or its constituent scales are related to treatment adherence (Harper et al., 1998; Lynch et al., 1992). In a study of exercise regimen adherence in hypercholesterolemic adults, only one scale (Premorbid Pessimism) of the eight core MBHI "coping" scales was related to adherence, and this was at only one of the three assessment periods (Lynch et al., 1992). A more recent study involving adherence among ninety cardiac transplant patients reported that lower scores on the Respectful coping style and Cooperative coping style scales and higher scores on the Sensitive coping style were all associated with poorer adherence prior to transplant, but these same scales were not uniquely related to treatment adherence following transplant (Harper et al., 1998). At this point, the utility of the MBHI as a tool to assess adherence-related personologic characteristics seems very limited.

Type A behavior pattern. Friedman and Rosenman (1974) first described the hard-driving, time-urgent, highly competitive, and hostile Type A behavioral style believed to be characteristic of individuals at risk for cardiovascular disease. Since this initial characterization the Type A behavior pattern (TABP) has received considerable attention as a potential risk factor for cardiovascular and other forms of physical disease (Matthews, 1988). Although the empirical evidence is not entirely consistent, reviews of the literature have generally concluded that the TABP is a reliable risk factor for the development of cardiovascular and possibly other physical diseases (Matthews, 1988; Miller et al., 1991). Most research and theorizing involving the Type A construct has focused on putative psychophysiologic pathways (e.g., greater cardiovascular responsivity to stress) as mediating an association between TABP and physical health. Suls and Sanders (1989) were among the first to suggest a behavioral model of Type A behavior and health; that is, that the tendency of Type A individuals toward cynicism, mistrust of others, and a generally hostile or oppositional style may precipitate nonadherence with medical advice, putting them at further risk for negative health outcomes. Similarly, Rhodewalt and Fairfield (1990) posited that patients exhibiting the Type A behavior pattern may be more likely to perceive medical regimens as threatening to their personal freedom and react with nonadherence in an attempt to regain perceived behavioral control. To date, however, little research has examined a possible association between TABP and adherence. Rhodewalt and Marcroft (1988) observed poorer metabolic control (presumably due to poorer regimen adherence) among insulin-dependent diabetic patients classified as Type A using the self-report Jenkins Activity Survey (JAS; Jenkins, Zyzanski, & Rosenman, 1979). However, other research has failed to find any association between the TABP and adherence (Cox et al., 1984; Lynch et al., 1992).

One possible explanation for the inconsistencies evident in past Type A research is the multifaceted nature of the global Type A behavior pattern, which includes components of competitiveness, time urgency, and hostility. Evidence from studies of more general health behavior suggests that the hostility component of the Type A pattern may be particularly relevant in this context. Higher scores on measures of hostility have been linked to reduced sleep and physical exercise, poor hygiene, and increased substance use (Smith, 1992). Little research to date has examined the association of individual differences in hostility with adherence. Christensen, Wiebe, & Lawton (1997) examined the role of hostility in predicting regimen adherence in a sample of forty-eight patients undergoing renal dialysis. Higher levels of hostility (defined using the Cook and Medley [1954] hostility scale) were associated with poorer medication and dietary adherence but were unrelated to an indicator of adherence to patients' restricted fluid-intake regimen. The effect of hostility on adherence was most pronounced among patients reporting the belief that positive health outcomes are not strongly related to the actions or advice of health care providers. The results of this single study suggest that individual differences in patient hostility may predict adherence to at least some treatment regimens and that the hostility construct warrants further attention from adherence researchers.

The Five-Factor Model of Personality

As past authors have argued, a lack of meaningful progress in research involving personologic predictors of health-related behavior in general (Smith & Williams, 1992) and treatment adherence specifically (Wiebe & Christensen, 1996) might, in part, be due to limitations in the way that personality is conceptualized and defined in health behavior research. The vast majority of studies involving personality factors and adherence have relied on measures that are, in many cases, not well defined or empirically validated. Further, without an organizing or taxonomic framework there is little understanding in this literature of the extent to which individual measures may overlap or may reflect common underlying personality dimensions.

The broader, more uniform, and empirically validated "Five-Factor Model" of personality may provide adherence researchers a useful framework to help guide in the identification of relevant personality traits for future research and in the interpretation of existing research. In contrast to many past methods of defining personality in the health behavior or adherence literatures, the Five-Factor Model has proved to be empirically reproducible in diverse populations, is defined using easily administered and objectively scored instruments, and reflects the normal range of variability in human personality rather than focusing on extreme or pathological characteristics (Digman, 1990; Costa & McCrae, 1992).

Decades of research and observation involving the lexical description of personality in written and spoken language has led to wide, though not universal, agreement that the tremendous heterogeneity in personality traits can be distilled to five core dimensions (Digman, 1990). The five dimensions include neuroticism (reflecting generalized emotional distress or chronic negative affect), extraversion (reflecting sociability, assertiveness, and cheerfulness), openness to experience (reflecting imaginativeness, intellectual curiosity, and unconventionality), agreeableness (reflecting altruism, trust of others' intentions and cooperativeness), and conscientiousness (reflecting self-discipline or self-control, dependability and will to achieve) (Digman, 1990). The five core domains of the model along with the thirty more specific personality facets that compose the higher-order domains as represented in the widely used NEO Personality Inventory (Costa & McCrae, 1992) are depicted in figure 3.1.

Most of the research involving the five-factor personality taxonomy and health-related behavior has focused on the traits of neuroticism and conscientiousness. Conscientiousness has proven to be the most consistent trait predictor of positive health practices and less risk-taking behavior in nonclinical samples (Booth-Kewley, & Vickers, 1994). The highly purposeful, self-disciplined style believed to characterize high conscientiousness scores also seems quite relevant to a patient's willingness and ability to comply with a prescribed treatment

---

The Five Factor Personality Model (Costa & McCrae, 1992)

Neuroticism
Anxiety
Angry hostility
Depression
Self-consciousness
Impulsiveness
Vulnerability

Agreeableness
Trust
Straightforwardness
Altruism
Compliance
Modesty
Tender-mindedness

Extraversion
Warmth
Gregariousness
Assertiveness
Activity
Excitement-seeking
Positive emotions

Conscientiousness
Competence
Order
Dutifulness
Achievement Striving
Self-discipline
Deliberation

Openness to Experience
Fantasy
Aesthetics
Feelings
Actions
Ideas
Values

Fig. 3.1. Core domains and personality facets of the Five-Factor Model of personality.

regimen (Wiebe & Christensen, 1996). Empirical evidence linking conscientiousness and adherence has been slow to accumulate. Christensen and Smith (1995) reported that higher conscientiousness was associated with more favorable dietary adherence in a sample of renal dialysis patients after the effects of relevant demographic variables were controlled. Rosenbaum & Ben-Ari Smira (1986) reported similar findings using the closely related individual difference dimension of learned resourcefulness. In contrast, a more recent investigation of treatment adherence among chronic dialysis patients failed to find an association between conscientiousness and treatment adherence (Moran, Christensen, & Lawton, 1997).

As is the case for lower conscientiousness, evidence suggests that individuals higher in trait neuroticism tend to engage in generally less positive health practices (Booth-Kewley & Vickers, 1994). Specific evidence concerning the relevance of neuroticism to treatment adherence is limited and mixed. A handful of studies have reported that patients higher in neuroticism exhibit poorer adherence to treatment (Delmonte, 1988; Evangelista, Berg, & Dracup, 2001; Wiebe et al., 1994). For example, in a study of eighty-two patients with congestive heart failure, higher neuroticism scores were found to be associated with significantly poorer medication, exercise, and clinic attendance adherence (Evangelista et al., 2001).

Other research has failed to find any association between the neuroticism trait and patient adherence (Christensen & Smith, 1995; Christensen, Moran, & Wiebe, 1999). Moreover, one recent study reported that higher levels of neuroticism are associated with more favorable adherence-related outcomes (i.e., better glycemic control among Type 2 diabetic patients) (Lane et al., 2000). Lane and colleagues interpreted this finding as suggesting that a proclivity toward more intense worry and negative emotionality may make the potential threat of uncontrolled diabetes more salient, resulting in additional motivation for a patient to more closely follow the treatment regimen.

In summary, there is modest, although not entirely consistent, evidence that higher levels of conscientiousness may distinguish adherent from nonadherent individuals. The evidence regarding neuroticism and adherence is more equivocal, with some studies reporting that higher neuroticism is associated with poorer adherence, some research reporting no relation, and at least one study reporting that higher neuroticism scores are associated with better treatment adherence.

In terms of the other core dimensions from the Five-Factor Model, little attempt has been made to document an association between extraversion, agreeableness, or openness to experience and adherence behavior. Circumscribed evidence exists linking these dimensions to health behavior differences. Higher agreeableness and extraversion have both been found to be associated with a more positive pattern of health practices, while high scores on the openness to experience trait have been linked to greater substance abuse (Booth-Kewley & Vickers, 1994). Past theorists have suggested that the hostile interpersonal style reflected by low agreeableness (or high antagonism) may be the component of the Type A behavior pattern that puts individuals at increased risk for cardiovascular and other diseases (Costa, McCrae, & Dembroski, 1989). Given that diminished treatment adherence is one likely pathway linking components of the Type A behavioral style with health outcomes, the potential link between the agreeableness disposition and adherence warrants special consideration in future research.

Locus of Control

Control-related beliefs have long played a central role as possible predictors of health-related behavior (Wallston & Wallston, 1982). The locus of control construct has had a particularly enduring impact on this literature for more than three decades (Strickland, 1978; Wallston, 1992). Individual differences in locus of control reflect the extent to which one believes that positive outcomes are due to one's own actions or behaviors or to some external factor or influence. The general locus of control construct (Rotter, 1966) was subsequently modified to reflect more specific control expectancies about health-related outcomes (Wallston, Wallston, & DeVellis, 1978). Since that time, the health locus of control construct has emerged as the single most frequently examined personologic variable in the adherence and health behavior literatures.

Despite extensive empirical attention, the association of locus of control and adherence behavior remains unclear (Wallston, 1992). Some evidence shows that patients with an internal locus of control (or internal *health* locus of control) exhibit more favorable adherence (Chen et al., 1999; McDonald-Miszczak, Maki, & Golud, 2000; Oldenburg, MacDonald, & Perkins, 1988; Poll & Kaplan De-Nour, 1980). However, other research suggests that internal control expectancies are not directly or significantly related to adherence (Brown & Fitzpatrick, 1988; Gravely & Oseasohn, 1991; Kaplan, Atkins, & Reinsch, 1984; McNaughton & Rodrigue, 2001; Schneider et al., 1991; Wittenberg et al., 1983). In a study involving a sample of 357 renal transplant patients, an internal health locus of control was found to be associated with *poorer* self-reported immunosuppressive medication adherence (Raiz et al., 1999). Also in this study, the belief that health outcomes are controlled by "powerful others" (i.e., health care providers) was associated with more favorable adherence. This latter finding is interesting in light of earlier work suggesting that, in some cases, a belief that care providers are centrally in control of patients' health outcomes (sometimes referred to as "vicarious" or "secondary" control) may be a more important determinant of adjustment and adherence than patients' personal or internal control beliefs (Christensen et al., 1996; Myers & Myers, 1999). This pattern has been most evident in treatment contexts where personal control over treatment delivery or treatment outcome may not be possible (see Reid, 1984).

Self-Efficacy

Patient individual differences in self-efficacy beliefs or expectancies reflect a psychological characteristic that has garnered substantial attention as a potential determinant of adherence behavior. Although many authors and researchers have failed to distinguish between locus of control and self-efficacy, these two constructs differ importantly. Locus of control refers to beliefs about whether obtaining a desired outcome (or avoiding an undesired outcome) is contingent upon one's own behavior (an outcome expectancy), and self-efficacy refers to the belief or expectancy that one possesses the ability to actually engage in or execute the behavior that is necessary to bring about that outcome (an efficacy expectancy). Thus, the two concepts are complementary and both may be important determinants of patient adherence.

Compared to findings involving locus of control and adherence, research regarding the role of self-efficacy in influencing adherence is consistent and robust. Considerable evidence suggests that situation-specific self-efficacy expectations are related to adherence across a range of treatment regimens (Brady et al., 1997; De Geest et al., 1995; Eitel et al., 1998; Ewart, 1992; Jensen et al., 1993; Kavanagh, Gooley, & Wilson, 1993). Most self-efficacy research, however, has relied on cross-sectional designs, making it difficult to establish the extent to which efficacy appraisals exert a causal influence on future adherence or are simply a consequence of past differences in adherence. A longitudinal study by Kavanagh et al. (1993) helped to clarify the causal pattern involved. In this study of sixty-three individuals with diabetes, those reporting high confidence that they could follow their treatment regimen over the next eight weeks exhibited more favorable adherence to the dietary, glucose testing, and exercise adherence guidelines over that time period (Kavanagh et al., 1993). Importantly, each of these significant effects remained significant after controlling for initial levels of adherence.

Other studies have found that adherence is best predicted through the joint consideration of locus of control expectancies and self-efficacy beliefs (Christensen et al., 1996; Kaplan et al., 1984). The idea that these two constructs may jointly predict adherence behavior is consistent with more general theorizing about social learning and social cognitive influences on behavior (Bandura, 1986). Consistent with this view, in a study involving exercise regimen adherence among sixty chronic obstructive pulmonary disease patients, Kaplan et al. (1984) reported that adherence was highest among patients with both strong self-efficacy beliefs and relatively strong internal health locus of control beliefs. Neither self-efficacy alone nor locus of control alone were significantly associated with adherence. The idea that both types of beliefs should be explicitly assessed and incorporated into predictive models of adherence appears promising and deserves further empirical attention.

Patient Depression

Patient emotional distress has long been considered a potential factor influencing treatment adherence. Depression may have particular relevance to adherence behaviors given that the experience of clinical depression is defined, in part, by motivational deficits, behavioral retardation, and cognitive slowing, all of which may impede the efforts or intentions of an individual that has been instructed to make systematic, sustained, and often demanding behavioral changes. Although considerable research has examined the potential relation of depression to treatment adherence, once again the pattern of findings is quite inconsistent. A number of studies involving chronic treatment regimens have failed to find a significant association between symptoms of depression, or negative mood more generally, and patient adherence (Carney et al., 1998; Christensen et al., 1994a; Friend et al., 1997; Botelho & Dudrak, 1992; Simoni et al., 1997). However, other research has documented a depression–adherence association (De-Nour & Czackes, 1976; de Groot et al., 1999; Littlefield et al., 1992; Ciechanowski, Katon, & Russo, 2000).

Both methodologic and treatment context or patient population differences may help to explain the inconsistency in this literature. For example, de Groot et al. (1999) found a strong significant association between patients having a history of major depression and glycemic control (a physiologic indicator influenced in part by adherence behavior) among individuals with Type 1 (insulin-dependent) diabetes. However, a history of depression was unrelated to glycemic control among individuals with the Type 2 (non-insulin-dependent) form of the disease. As de Groot and colleagues point out, the treatments for these two conditions can differ substantially. Type 2 diabetes is usually treated with oral medications and dietary changes. Type 1 diabetes requires a more demanding self-care regimen including regular insulin injections. Depressed patients may have particular difficulty managing the more rigorous behavioral requirements usually required in the treatment of Type 1 diabetes.

A second important issue to consider in evaluating the results of depression studies involves the way that depression was defined in a particular investigation. Studies that utilized self-report measures of depression symptoms have typically observed a different pattern of results than investigations that classify patients according to a formal diagnostic assessment. To the extent that depression is related to non-adherence, it is likely to be the neurovegetative states (e.g., reduced motivation, fatigability, behavioral retardation) seen in clinical depression that are responsible for the relationship. These more severe symptoms are not as likely to be present among individuals simply reporting mood changes or other subclinical depressive symptoms on a self-report measure. This interpretation is consistent with the findings of a review of the statistical effects reported in studies examining depression and glycemic control among patients with diabetes (Lustman et al., 2000). The average effect of depression on diabetic control was greater in studies using standardized clinical interview assessments and criteria-based diagnoses of depression than in studies relying on self-report measures of depressive symptoms.

In sum, findings from research involving the association of depression and adherence are inconsistent. The strength of the association varies across patient and medical treatment subgroups and as a function of how depression is defined. Depression is most likely to play a role among more severely or clinically depressed patients who are managing medical regimens that pose substantial or complex self-care demands.

Social Support and the Social Environment

Considerable evidence in a range of medical treatment populations suggests that the availability and perceived quality of social support are important correlates of regimen adherence (e.g., Christensen et al., 1992; Finnegan & Suler, 1985; Catz et al., 2000; Kulik & Mahler, 1993; Levy, 1983; Stanton, 1987). For example, in a prospective study of fifty individuals being treated for hypertension, greater perceived satisfaction with support providers was associated with better medication regimen adherence as determined by pill counts and a higher percentage of kept medical appointments (Stanton, 1987). Similar results have been reported among patients undergoing treatment for diabetes (Hanson, Henggeler, & Burghen, 1987), individuals recovering from coronary artery bypass graft surgery (Kulik & Mahler, 1993), and HIV-positive individuals being treated with complex medication regimens (Catz et al., 2000). Some evidence shows that the salutary effect of support on adherence is strongest among patients who have recently experienced a high degree of life stress (Griffith, Field, & Lustman, 1990). This pattern is consistent with the stress-buffering model of social support in which available or perceived support becomes more important for an individual's well-being as the degree of stress the individual is experiencing increases (Cohen & Wills, 1985).

There is again inconsistency in the available research findings, however. Other studies have found that social support was not related, or was inconsistently related to adherence to various chronic treatment regimens (Boyer et al., 1990; Hitchcock et al., 1992; Rudman, Gonzales, Borgida, 1999; Sherbourne et al., 1992). A few studies have even reported greater support to be associated with poorer treatment adherence (Funch & Gale, 1986; Kaplan & Hartwell, 1987; Moran et al., 1997). Kaplan and Hartwell (1987) suggested that individuals with larger social networks are more likely to face social situations or obligations that may pose a barrier to treatment adherence. Similarly, for some individuals increased social contact may give rise to a greater degree of perceived social stigma surrounding medication taking or dietary choices. As Moran and colleagues (1997) have discussed, potential social barriers to adherence may be most likely to occur for treatments that involve changes in dietary or drinking behavior, both of which are strongly influenced by social factors (cf. Redd & de Castro, 1992).

Some evidence indicates that the effect of perceived social support or the size of one's social network on adherence may differ according to gender (Kaplan & Hartwell, 1987; Kimmel et al., 1995). The collective findings from these two studies do not add significant clarity, however, because very different patterns were observed. Kimmel et al. (1995) reported that greater perceived support has beneficial effects on adherence among male renal dialysis patients but not among female patients. In contrast, Kaplan & Hartwell (1987) reported greater support satisfaction to be associated with better diabetic control among women but poorer control among men. On a second measure of social support (reflecting the size of one's identifiable social network) a larger social network was associated with less success in either completing or benefiting from a diabetes self-management group for both genders (Kaplan & Hartwell, 1987).

As past authors have proposed, perceived family support or characteristics of the patient's family environment may play a particularly important role in regard to patient adjustment or adherence, especially among individuals facing serious chronic disease (Christensen et al., 1989; Dimond, 1979; Kerns & Weiss, 1994; Turk & Kerns, 1985). For example, in our own work involving patients with end-stage renal disease who are undergoing renal dialysis, a more supportive family environment characterized by greater cohesion and expressiveness among family members and less intrafamily conflict exhibited significantly more favorable adherence to fluid-intake restrictions than patients reporting less family support (Christensen et al., 1992).

Although there are fewer available studies involving social or familial factors and adherence among pediatric patients, at least two have reached a similar conclusion. Davis et al. (1996) reported better post-transplantation adherence among pediatric patients whose parents were classified as having more favorable verbal and nonverbal communication skills. In a study involving somewhat older children, greater perceived parental support on the part of the child was associated with better adherence to several specific aspects of the self-care regimen as well as better glycemic control among this sample of adolescents with insulin-dependent diabetes (Hanson, Henggler, & Burgehn, 1987).

In summary, although the evidence involving social support and adherence is not entirely consistent, there is compelling evidence that greater perceived support satisfaction (or qualitative aspects of support) is associated with more favorable adherence to at least some aspects of medical treatment regimens. The association between adherence and the size of a patient's available social network (or other quantitative aspects of support) is much less clear. Moreover, there is some indication that social contact may pose a barrier to adherence in some cases. Although less research has examined the importance of familial support or specific characteristics of a patient's family environment, these factors may have particularly important effects on patient adherence, especially for individuals following chronic treatment regimens. Finally, the issue of whether the effects of social support differ according to gender remains unclear and requires further investigation.

Provider Characteristics and the Interpersonal Nature of Health Care

Medical treatment delivery is, at its core, an interpersonal enterprise. Central to this enterprise is the health care provider–patient dyad. For effective and safe treatment delivery to proceed, several dyadic qualities and relationship processes must be present. First and foremost, there must be effective, bidirectional communication and information exchange between provider and patient (DiMatteo, 1998). Without clarity, veridicality, and completeness in the exchange of information, the providers' ability to implement an appropriate treatment is impaired, and the ability and willingness of the patient to adhere to the treatment regimen is compromised. There must also be a degree of mutual trust shared by patient and provider (Caterinicchio, 1979; Thom, 2001). A patient seeking health care must trust that the provider possesses the ability and intention to act in the patient's best interests. The provider must in turn trust that patient reports are accurate to the degree necessary to make clinically appropriate diagnostic and treatment decisions, and the provider must feel confident in the premise that a prescribed intervention will be carried out by the patient as implemented. Finally, provider–patient interactions must involve a careful and conscious balancing of the roles and responsibilities of patient and provider. Although some degree of deference to the expertise and authority afforded the provider is needed, maintaining the autonomy and self-determination of the patient is equally important (Haug, 1997; Stone, 1979).

Each provider–patient exchange, each treatment decision, and the successful execution of each treatment plan necessarily involves two, arguably coequal, players. However, the relative contribution of patient and provider at the various stages of health-related transactions have not typically been construed equally. Up to the point that a diagnosis is made and a treatment regimen is formulated and prescribed, both historical and contemporary medical education and practice underscores the central, dominant role of the provider (Parsons, 1954; Goldstein et al., 1987). Beyond the point that a treatment is prescribed, however, there is an outright shift in responsibility from the provider to the patient, who is expected to carry out the regimen, often with no additional input or support from the practitioner. Both of these traditions reflect extremes. Just as neglecting the role of the patient in the earlier stages of a health transaction may impede the formulation of a clinically appropriate treatment plan, ignoring the role or potential role of the provider in influencing whether a treatment regimen or therapeutic recommendation is actually carried out by the patient once he or she leaves the clinical setting is similarly insufficient.

Provider and Practice Style Characteristics and Patient Adherence

The relation of provider or practice characteristics to patient adherence has been afforded little attention in the research literature. Few characteristics have been considered, and even fewer have been identified as clearly important. The most comprehensive examination of physician characteristics as potential determinants of patient satisfaction and treatment adherence was carried out as part of the large, multisite Medical Outcomes Study (DiMatteo et al., 1993). This two-year longitudinal study included a demographically diverse group of 186 physicians representing a range of medical specialties and treating a variety of patient groups. Adherence to a number of different treatment-related behaviors was assessed (medication taking, exercise, diet); however, all adherence measures were limited by a reliance on patient self-report.

No significant associations were found between demographic characteristics of the physician (e.g., gender, age, ethnicity) and adherence. A number of intriguing findings related to provider practice style and practice characteristics were revealed, however. For example, the provider's self-reported willingness to fully answer all of the patient's questions was positively related to adherence to exercise recommendations. The effect of this aspect of practice style, however, was unrelated to several other adherence indices. This inconsistency is mirrored in other studies involving the association between information provision and patient adherence. In their quantitative review of the available literature on provider–patient interaction, Hall, Roter, and Katz (1988) found that greater information provision on the part of the provider was associated with greater patient satisfaction but not clearly linked to patient adherence.

An issue that is often discussed as having a potentially negative impact on patient outcomes involves the limited amount of time many providers afford their individual patients. The stereotype of the rushed, harried physician who faces the daily prospect of seeing an ever-increasing number of patients in an ever-decreasing amount of time is widely held. Examinations of physician practice characteristics suggest that, more often than not, this stereotype is accurate. A study of more than 3,000 patient visits conducted by more than 100 different family practice physicians (who have an arguably more holistic perspective than other specialties) found that the average amount of time spent with each patient was just over ten minutes (Zyzanski et al., 1998). No measure of regimen adherence was obtained in this study. Interestingly, however, other research has found no clear evidence that routinely shorter visits are associated with poorer adherence (DiMatteo et al., 1993).

Although the amount of time that providers spend with individual patients has not been linked to adherence differences, a growing body of evidence does suggest that certain qualitative aspects of provider–patient interactions are quite important. For example, more positive verbal comments or communications (e.g., reassurance, support, encouragement) and fewer negative communications (e.g., anger, criticism, anxiety) during the appointment are associated with better patient adherence (Hall et al., 1988). Other research suggests that the amount of time spent "chatting" with patients about nonmedical topics is strongly associated with patient satisfaction even after controlling for visit length (Gross et al., 1998).

An interesting finding of the DiMatteo study was that medication adherence was better among patients of physicians who saw *more* patients per week. DiMatteo and colleagues interpreted this as reflecting either differences in physician "popularity" (i.e., patients may have been more likely to follow the instruction of the better-liked or more popular providers) or as reflecting the possibility that providers with busier practices saw individual patients more frequently. Consistent with this latter interpretation was another finding in this study that patients reported more favorable adherence if definite follow-up appointments were made after they were initially seen for treatment. Finally, after controlling for baseline adherence ratings, physicians' ratings of their own overall job satisfaction significantly predicted future adherence among their patients. Job satisfaction has certainly been associated with job performance in a number of occupations (e.g., Cropanzo & Wright, 2001). This intriguing finding suggests that in the case of medical care delivery, the effects of provider morale extend to patient behavior outside the clinic or office setting. Identifying precisely what it is about physician job satisfaction that promotes adherence among patients requires further investigation.

In summary, a modest amount of research and few consistent findings are available regarding the potential role of physician or physician practice characteristics in influencing patient adherence. There is evidence that more positive (and fewer negative) communications and affective expressions on the part of the provider are associated with more favorable patient adherence as is more time devoted to nonmedical "chatting" with patients. In contrast to conventional wisdom, the associations between adherence and the amount of information providers give to patients, and the amount of time spent in individual patient visits, are both equivocal. What is clear, however, is that provider determinants of adherence have been largely ignored in both the descriptive and empirical literatures and that the resulting lack of information greatly compromises our ability to understand and to facilitate patient treatment adherence.

Moving Forward: Conceptual and Methodologic Issues in Adherence Research

As the current chapter has made clear, empirical progress in research involving determinants or predictors of patient adherence has been slow, and reported data have lacked consistency across studies, across clinical populations, and between different regimen types. As noted above, research conducted over the past four decades involving personality and adherence has been limited by the lack of a common organizing framework or structural theory to guide the assessment of personality. Although no particular taxonomy for personality assessment has been unanimously upheld, there is an emerging consensus that the Five-Factor Model of personality can provide the type of structure and direction that adherence researchers need better to understand past findings and, more importantly, to articulate and test new theory-driven hypotheses about individual differences in adherence behavior.

Another conceptual or theoretical consideration involves the fact that most adherence research has examined only the direct or main effects of patient characteristics on adherence. For example, many studies have hypothesized that a particular personality trait is, in general, "adaptive" in terms of adherence. Past research has generally ignored the possibility that the associations between personality (or other psychosocial variables) and patient adherence may be more accurately viewed from a perspective that considers the interaction of patient individual differences with disease and treatment-related contextual factors (the *patient-by-context interactive perspective*). In other words, the relation of a particular patient factor to treatment adherence might expectedly vary as a function of differences in the illness context or between study sample differences in the treatment regimen itself. The utility of an interactionalist perspective for better understanding adherence determinants is taken up in detail in chapter 4.

From a methodologic perspective, one of the most important limitations of adherence research has involved a reliance on cross-sectional research designs. Relying on concurrent assessments of both personologic factors and adherence makes causal interpretations difficult or impossible. For example, when an association between adherence and patient self-efficacy beliefs has been observed in cross-sectional research, it has not been possible to determine with any certainty the extent to which differences in self-efficacy actually preceded and led to a change in adherence. Alternatively, past experiences with the treatment regimen may have been responsible for a change in efficacy beliefs, or self-efficacy and adherence may have reciprocally influenced each other or been mutually influenced by a third variable.

Causal interpretations in research involving chronic disorders is most difficult because the assessment of patient characteristics is confounded with the patient's current medical condition, treatment history, and past experiences with the treatment regimen. Ideally, research designs would include "premorbid" patient assessments before the individual actually becomes symptomatic and requires medical intervention. Unfortunately, researchers have few opportunities to assess patients prior to the onset of the illness of interest. One option is to utilize general population or community-based sampling in an effort to identify an adequate number of individuals who will eventually develop a particular medical problem requiring a particular type of treatment. This strategy obviously requires tremendous investment of time and resources in an effort to obtain an adequate number of at-risk individuals. The total sample must then be followed long enough for a small subgroup of individuals to develop a particular medical problem and require treatment for the problem.

Certain conditions have precursors making the identification of a truly high-risk sample more feasible. For example, patients with progressive renal insufficiency can often be identified based on routine laboratory screening months or even years before the patient develops related symptoms or requires medical intervention. In other cases, highly predictive genetic markers have been used to identify high-risk subpopulations. For example, women testing positive for the so-called breast cancer genes (the BRCA-1 or BRCA-2 genes) are at significantly higher risk for the development of breast and ovarian cancers than are other women with a family history of the disease. Reported data suggest that women with both a family history of breast cancer and the defective BRCA-1 gene have an 85 percent chance of developing breast cancer and a 63 percent chance of developing ovarian cancer by age seventy (Easton, Ford, Bishop, 1995). In Huntington's Disease (HD) the genetic marker is even more closely tied to disease development. There is a 5 percent chance of passing on the mutated HD gene to one's offspring. Individuals with the faulty gene are then certain to develop the disorder, usually in mid-adulthood. Continuing advances in mapping the human genome are likely to make the identification of specific high-risk groups more feasible. A by-product of these efforts is likely to be a unique opportunity for adherence researchers (as well as researchers interested in adaptation to disease more broadly) to identify and assess at-risk individuals before symptoms develop and prior to the initiation of treatment (at which time patient predispositions and treatment or illness factors can become highly confounded). At-risk individuals could then be followed over time until treatment is ultimately implemented and adherence to treatment is assessed, avoiding many of the interpretative problems inherent in other research designs.

In Conclusion

Patient nonadherence clearly poses a significant risk to treatment effectiveness in virtually all treatment domains and clinical populations. Explicitly evaluating information about patient individual difference characteristics and social or environmental characteristics believed to influence adherence, and incorporating this information into treatment decision-making and patient risk stratification schemes, has the potential to impact clinical outcomes in many ways. Achieving this impact, however, will require additional investigation, refinement in research methodologies, broader thinking about potential determinants of patient adherence, and ultimately will require a concerted effort to translate findings from adherence research into standard patient assessment and medical practice paradigms.

4

An Interactive Framework for Adherence Research and Practice

As the first three chapters of this book have made clear, associations between patient psychological characteristics and adherence behavior lack consistency across studies, measures, and study populations. This lack of consistency has been interpreted by past authors as suggesting that patient characteristics (e.g., personality differences, coping style, patient beliefs) do not play a predictable or important role as determinants of adherence behavior (e.g., Haynes, 1979; Kaplan & Simon, 1990; Meichenbaum & Turk, 1987; Dunbar-Jacob & Schlenk, 2001). This conclusion may be overly pessimistic. Over the past ten years my colleagues and I have been accumulating evidence to support an alternative interpretation of the admittedly disappointing data that have accumulated concerning determinants of patient adherence (Christensen, 2000; Christensen et al., 1994a; Wiebe & Christensen, 1996). This alternative view rests on the premise that the adaptive significance of a particular patient characteristic in regard to treatment regimen adherence may, to a large degree, depend upon the specific requirements or characteristics of the regimen itself. In other words, what "works" for patients in some treatment-related situations might not be adaptive in other contexts.

My general contention is that we can better understand how psychological factors influence adherence if we adopt a perspective that considers the joint or interactive effects of patient factors along with characteristics of the chronic illness and medical treatment context (the *person X context interactive perspective*). In contrast to this interactive view, the vast majority of adherence studies conducted over the past four decades have relied on a main-effect or bivariate approach to conceptualizing and empirically examining psychological correlates or determinants of adherence behavior. For example, many studies have examined the main-effect or bivariate association between individual differences in locus of control expectancies and adherence to various medical treatment regimens. As is the case for research involving nearly all other hypothesized determinants of adherence, results have been mixed. Some of these studies have found a positive association between higher internal control expectancies and better adherence (e.g., Chen et al., 1999; McDonald-Miszczak, Maki, & Gould, 2000), while other studies have reported either that locus of control is unrelated to adherence or that stronger internal control beliefs may actually be associated with poorer adherence among some patient subgroups (e.g., McNaughton & Rodrigue, 2001; Raiz et al., 1999). In relying on an overly simplistic, mechanistic view of the associations between psychological characteristics and adherence, these "main-effect studies" have ignored the tremendous heterogeneity that exists among patients with different types of physical disease, varying prognoses and physical symptom patterns, and undergoing different types of medical intervention. Most importantly, studies of this type have failed to consider the possibility that the association between patient characteristics and regimen adherence might be expected to vary as a function of one or more aspects of the chronic illness and medical treatment context.

An Interactionalist View

At a general level the person-by-context interactive framework has a long history in the science of psychology. In the 1970s an "interactionalist" perspective emerged as a popular alternative to the long-standing debate concerning personologic versus situational influences on behavior (Higgins, 1990). From this perspective, attempts to identify personality traits or dispositions that predict behavior are of limited usefulness without also considering the situation or context an individual is facing. As Bem and Funder (1978, pp. 485–486) asserted, "it is the interaction between the person and the situation that supplies most of the psychologically interesting variance in behavior."

Within clinical psychology, the interactionalist perspective has been most commonly applied in the psychotherapy outcome research literature (Dance & Neufeld, 1988). Psychotherapy outcome studies that have adopted an interactive perspective consider the possibility that a given intervention strategy may be more effective for certain subgroups of patients. This approach serves as an alternative to the common practice of treating all patients with a given disorder or target problem as a homogenous group, ignoring potentially important patient differences (Beutler, 1991). One of the more consistent patterns that has emerged from the psychotherapy outcome literature is that individuals with more active and internally focused coping styles show a better response to interventions that emphasize self-control rather than therapist control (Dance & Neufeld, 1988). For example, in research involving treatments for weight reduction, individuals scoring higher on a measure of self-reinforcement tendencies exhibited higher weight loss when undergoing an intervention that stressed patient direction and self-control rather than therapist control. The opposite pattern was observed for patients scoring low in self-reinforcement tendencies (Rozensky & Bellack, 1976). Thus, the degree of congruence between patients' characteristic style of coping and the nature of the intervention utilized was an important predictor of treatment outcome.

Interactions between individual difference variables and health-related interventions and outcomes have been most consistently demonstrated in studies of psychological preparations for stressful medical procedures (Schultheis, Peterson, & Selby, 1987). In general, this research also suggests that the degree of congruence between characteristics of the intervention and patient coping style is an important determinant of outcome. For example, the provision of detailed procedural and sensory information to patients prior to undergoing a stressful procedure appears to facilitate adjustment for patients with an active or approach-oriented coping focus who characteristically monitor stress-relevant information in a vigilant manner. For patients with less vigilant or more avoidant orientations, however, information-based intervention typically either has no effect or has a deleterious impact on adjustment (Martelli et al., 1987; Miller & Mangan, 1983). Conversely, those patients possessing a less vigilant or avoidant coping style seem to exhibit more positive outcomes when provided less-specific information about an impending procedure or interventions that divert attention from the procedure (e.g., distraction, relaxation training). Despite these applications of person X context models in various areas of psychology and health care, until recently there have been relatively few attempts to study patient adherence behavior from an interactive perspective.

The Illness and Medical Treatment Context

The fundamental components of the patient X context interactive framework as applied to regimen adherence are illustrated in figure 4.1. The dashed lines reflect the fact that significant main effects between patient characteristics or contextual factors and adherence are often not consistently found, and the emboldened line reflects the importance the model places on the interactive effects of patient and contextual factors. The central assumption in the model is that relevant contextual or situational features should be explicitly assessed, and the interaction of these factors with patient variables tested directly.

A challenge implicit in the interactive model involves the fact that there are innumerable illness or medical treatment characteristics that could potentially be considered within an interactive framework. The specific contextual factors that are most relevant to the psychological characteristics being considered, or to the adherence process itself, may not always be obvious. A "contextual taxonomy" of sorts is needed to help guide the application of the model to the highly heterogeneous and complex medical illness and treatment context. As a conceptual starting point, I believe the broader literature on psychological stress and the effects of stress can be very helpful in this regard. Many contextual aspects of the illness and medical treatment context (see figure

4.2) mirror those characteristics of stressful encounters that have been identified as being important moderators of how stress affects the individual physiologically, emotionally, and behaviorally (Frankenhauser, 1975; Glass & Singer, 1972). For example, it is clear from the more general stress literature that controllable stressors affect an individual quite differently than do stressors that are beyond one's control. Just as stressor controllability varies widely in other domains, degree of patient control differs widely across different illness and treatment groups or subgroups. Some medical interventions (e.g., diabetic management) allow or require a high degree of patient direction or treatment-related control, while other interventions (e.g., most forms of cancer treatment) allow considerably less opportunity for patient control or involvement in treatment delivery. Similarly, just as the predictability or ambiguity of non-health-related stressful encounters is known to have important implications for the effects of stress, medical disorders themselves differ in the terms of the predictability of symptom patterns or in the ambiguity of patient prognoses. Even short-term variability in symptom severity can be unpredictable in some conditions (e.g., rheumatoid arthritis) and relatively more predictable in others (e.g., cardiovascular disease). From the patient X context perspective one would not necessarily expect that the same associations between personologic differences and adherence be observed across such disparate contexts. As an example, consider the association between the locus of control construct and adherence. The adaptive significance of locus of control in regard to adherence might be expected to vary as a function of the specific requirements or demands of the treatment regimen that the patient is instructed to follow. The lack of consistency across heterogeneous treatment settings and populations observed in many studies might be interpreted as an expression of person X context interactive behavioral patterns that expectedly vary across differing contexts.

Applying the Interactive Framework: An Illustration from Research Involving End-Stage Renal Disease

A series of studies conducted by my colleagues and me involving patients with end-stage renal disease (ESRD) has illustrated the potential

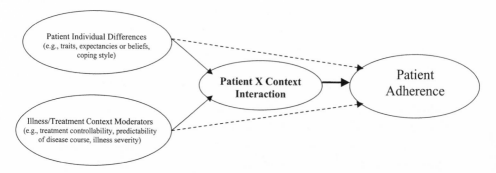

Fig. 4.1. Conceptual representation of the patient X context interactive framework.

The Illness and Medical Treatment Context

Controllability
Patient versus provider control over
   treatment delivery
Control over illness course/treatment
Control over treatment decision-making

Predictability
Ambiguity of patient prognosis
Predictability of symptom patterns
Predictability of treatment outcome

Stressor Intensity
Degree of illness-related functional impairment
Degree of co-morbidity
Symptom burden

Fig. 4.2. Examples of contextual characteristics of medical treatments and medical disorders.

value of the interactive framework in understanding influences on adherence behavior (e.g., Christensen et al., 1990; Christensen et al., 1994a; Christensen, 2000). Upon the cessation of kidney function, the over 300,000 ESRD patients in the United States must undergo lifelong medical therapy to stay alive. Available treatments for ESRD include renal transplantation and several forms of renal dialysis. Given a shortage of donor organs and a significant transplant rejection rate, the large majority of ESRD patients rely on some form of renal dialysis as treatment for their condition. The primary renal dialysis modalities are hemodialysis ("center" or "home") and peritoneal dialysis. There is an important distinction in the role taken by the patient while undergoing the different forms of medical treatment. In center hemodialysis, the patient maintains a very passive role. There is typically little that patients are required or even allowed to do in terms of actively participating in hemodialysis treatment delivery. The center hemodialysis procedure is performed three times a week by nurses or renal technicians in a hospital or clinic setting, requiring approximately four hours per session. Hemodialysis treatment involves establishing a vascular connection between the dialysis machine and the patient, usually through an arteriovenous fistula (a vascular access composed of both an artery and a vein) surgically created in the patient's forearm. During the procedure a high volume of blood is circulated through an artificial kidney, allowing excess fluid and toxins to be removed.

For some patients the hemodialysis procedure is carried out at home. Although home and center hemodialysis are essentially the same from a biomedical and mechanical standpoint, there are key behavioral differences. Home hemodialysis patients have the opportunity to be much more actively involved in treatment delivery and direction. Home hemodialysis patients typically are responsible for their own needle insertion, administering necessary medications, and monitoring their own vital signs as well as various vital functions of the dialysis machine. Moreover, home dialysis patients have considerably less frequent contact with renal care providers and are able to set and maintain their own dialysis schedules. In contrast to their center hemodialysis counterparts, home patients clearly play a more central and behaviorally involved role in dialysis treatment delivery.

Peritoneal dialysis treatment typically requires the patient to take an even more active role to ensure treatment success in what is a behaviorally complex protocol. In continuous ambulatory peritoneal dialysis (CAPD), the most common form of peritoneal dialysis treatment, a permanent catheter is surgically implanted in the abdomen. The patient uses a sterile tube to connect the catheter to a bag of sterile dialysis solution (dialysate). The bag is elevated to allow flow of the dialysate into the abdominal cavity. After this procedure is completed the bag is tucked away under the patient's clothing. Over the next four to eight hours the patient remains ambulatory as continuous dialysis ensues. During this "dwell time," blood filters through the peritoneal membrane leaving toxins and excess fluid behind in the solution. After the dwell time is complete, the patient repositions the bag and the used solution is allowed to drain back into the bag, where it is discarded and the procedure begins again. Throughout each step of the procedure the patient must remain vigilant about keeping themselves and the dialysis connections sterile to help avoid serious infection that can begin at the catheter access site. As is the case with home hemodialysis, peritoneal dialysis patients have relatively infrequent contact with health care providers and are able to control their own dialysis schedules. The successful administration of peritoneal dialysis is clearly dependent on the patient taking a more active and directive role in his or her treatment relative to patients undergoing center hemodialysis.

In general, the choice of a particular ESRD treatment modality is substantially influenced by nonmedical factors, including patient and provider preferences and judgments about which modality might be associated with the most favorable patient adherence (Christensen & Moran, 1998; Davison, 1996; Wing, 1984). In fact, center hemodialysis, home hemodialysis, and peritoneal dialysis are all medically acceptable treatment alternatives for the large majority of patients. Accordingly, the availability of a number of different treatment contexts in ESRD, each with a different set of patient demands and clearly differing in terms of the degree of behavioral control patients are afforded, offers a unique opportunity to apply an interactive framework to study patient outcomes.

In addition to undergoing the dialysis treatment itself, patients are required to adhere to a multifaceted behavioral regimen that includes making multiple dietary changes, following fluid-intake restrictions, and adhering to one or more medication regimens. Not adhering to these aspects of the dialysis regimen carries a substantial risk of severe complications. For example, a failure to limit fluid intake can result in congestive heart failure and can exacerbate hypertension, and a failure to modify diet through limited consumption of phosphorus-rich and potassium-rich foods can lead to serious bone disease (due to elevated serum phosphorus levels) and potentially fatal cardiac arrhythmia (due to elevated serum potassium levels). Despite the severity of the threats associated with nonadherence, the available data suggest that between 30 and 50 percent of dialysis patients do not adhere to diet, fluid-intake, and medication regimens (Bame, Petersen, &

Wray, 1993; Christensen et al., 1992; Schneider et al., 1991; Wolcott et al., 1986).

From the perspective of the patient X context model, adherence is expected to be best when the patient's characteristic or preferred style of coping is consistent with the contextual features or behavioral demands of the particular type of dialysis treatment the patient is undergoing (Christensen & Moran, 1998). In an early study (Christensen et al., 1990) we tested this premise in a sample of fifty-three patients undergoing either provider-directed center hemodialysis or patient-directed home hemodialysis. Each patient's characteristic or preferred style of coping was assessed using the "preference for behavioral involvement scale" from the Krantz Health Opinion Survey (Krantz, Baum, & Wideman, 1980). Scores on this scale reflect the degree to which a patient desires active involvement in his or her own medical treatment and prefers self-care over care administered by a health care provider. Consistent with the interactive model, among patients undergoing center hemodialysis, higher scores on the preference for behavioral involvement scale were associated with significantly worse dietary adherence (reflected by higher serum potassium levels). In contrast, for patients undergoing hemodialysis at home, patients with strong preferences for active involvement displayed better dietary adherence. Thus, adherence was best explained by the degree of congruency between patient coping style or coping preference and the levels of involvement permitted or required by the particular treatment patients received.

In a somewhat later study (Christensen et al., 1994a), we examined dialysis regimen adherence among fifty-two staff-treated center hemodialysis patients and thirty-four self-treated CAPD patients. Patient coping style was assessed using a multivariate composite variable (labeled "information vigilance") of five self-report individual difference scales or subscales; the "preference for behavioral involvement" and "preference for information" subscales from the KHOS, the Miller Behavioral Styles Scale (Miller & Mangan, 1983), and the internal and powerful others health locus of control subscales from the Multidimensional Health Locus of Control scale (Wallston et al., 1978). Each of these component measures was significantly intercorrelated, and each reflects individual differences in the tendency or motivation of patients to exercise personal control in health contexts and/or to actively attend to threat-relevant information related to health and treatment.

As depicted in figure 4.3, after controlling for patient age, disease duration, and years of education, higher scores on the composite information vigilance dimension were associated with better dietary adherence (lower serum potassium levels) for self-treated CAPD patients, but poorer dietary adherence (higher serum potassium levels) for center hemodialysis patients. In contrast, low information vigilance was associated with better dietary adherence for staff-treated cen-

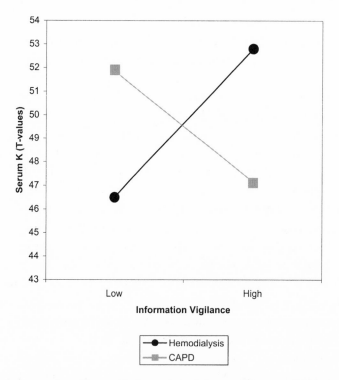

Fig. 4.3. Interactive effects of information vigilance and type of dialysis (i.e., CAPD versus center hemodialysis) on dietary adherence (serum K levels). Serum K values were standardized (into *T* scores) within each dialysis treatment group. From Christensen et al. (1994).

ter hemodialysis patients, but poorer dietary adherence for CAPD patients. These findings again suggest that the degree of congruence between the patient's coping style and the self-care demands of a prescribed medical treatment is an important determinant of adherence.

Prospective Study of the Interactive Framework

As noted in previous chapters, one of the most common limitations of adherence research in general involves a common reliance on cross-sectional research designs. Causal interpretations in cross-sectional research involving chronic disorders is particularly difficult because the assessment of patient characteristics is confounded with the patient's current medical condition, treatment history, and past experiences with the treatment regimen. Ideally, researchers would obtain a premorbid assessment of patients on the variables of interest. As chronic illness researchers are well aware, however, the prospect of identifying "at-risk" patients before disease onset is a challenging proposition in most patient populations.

In an attempt to address some of the limitations inherent in earlier cross-sectional research, we examined the interactive framework in a sample of patients at an early, asymptomatic stage in the progression of renal insufficiency (Christensen, Moran, & Ehlers, 1999). For the majority of patients with chronic renal failure, end-stage renal disease is the end result of a progressive deterioration in kidney function over a period of months or years. Identifying future ESRD patients who are at an early stage of renal insufficiency provided a unique opportunity to prospectively test hypotheses concerning the prediction of adherence to a future regimen.

In this preliminary study we identified sixty-nine patients for whom routine laboratory screening had revealed evidence of mild to moderate renal insufficiency. All patients were believed to have a form of progressive renal disease and were enrolled in the present study when their serum creatinine levels (a general marker of renal function) reached 3.5 mg/dl or greater. Patients were reassessed approximately twenty-four months after the initial assessment. At follow-up, twenty-nine of the patients were being treated with staff-directed center hemodialysis, and fourteen were being treated with self-managed home hemodialysis. Nine patients were undergoing other forms of treatment and were not included in the analysis due to the limited sample size of these subgroups. Disease status in the remaining seventeen patients had not progressed to the point that renal dialysis was required.

Our primary hypothesis in this study was that the patients' level of information vigilance assessed in the early, asymptomatic stage of renal insufficiency would interact with the type of renal dialysis eventually prescribed in predicting adherence. The primary adherence measure consisted of mean interdialysis session weight gain (an indicator of fluid-intake adherence) averaged over four weeks (twelve dialysis sessions). Interdialysis weight gain (IWG) is obtained by subtracting the postdialysis weight for the previous treatment session from the predialysis weight for the current session. The values resulting from this computation are believed to be a valid reflection of the amount of fluid that the patient ingests between treatment sessions (Manley & Sweeney, 1986). Higher IWG values are interpreted as reflecting poorer patient adherence, with values over 2.5 kg generally indicative of problematic adherence.

Among home hemodialysis patients, those reporting higher information vigilance scores at the pre-ESRD assessment displayed better adherence (lower mean IWG) relative to low information vigilance patients (see figure 4.4). In contrast, among center hemodialysis patients, higher information vigilance was associated with poorer adherence to the fluid-intake regimen.

It is important to note that in each of the interactive studies reviewed (Christensen et al., 1990; 1994a; 1999), we obtained no main or direct effects for any of the patient individual difference variables we considered. However, the statistical interaction between coping style and treatment type was significant in each case. In other words, had we limited our study design to an examination of patient characteristics without explicitly considering the specific type of medical treatment patients were undergoing, we would have concluded that none of the individual difference measures we examined were significantly associated with regimen adherence. Examining the interaction of patient and context led to a very different conclusion.

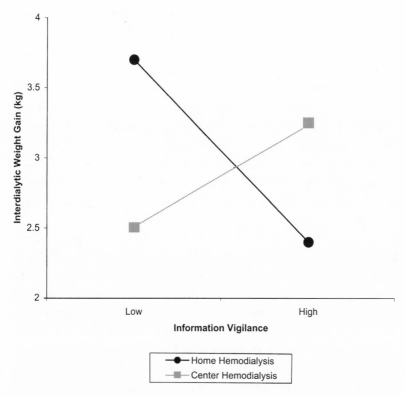

Fig. 4.4. Interactive effects of information vigilance and type of dialysis (center versus home hemodialysis) on adherence with fluid-intake restrictions (mean interdialytic weight gain). From Christensen (2000).

Further Applications of the Interactive Framework to the Study of Adherence

Relevance of the framework to other patient characteristics. Most of the research involving the patient X context framework conducted thus far has involved coping style or coping preference measures. A variety of other individual difference characteristics are also conceptually relevant to the framework. The association between these characteristics and adherence might also be clarified through application of the interactive framework. For example, individual differences in perceived self-efficacy might be more relevant to adherence among patients undergoing medical treatments that require a high degree of patient independence or control. The interactive framework might also integrate dimensions from the Five-Factor Model of personality (see Christensen & Johnson, 2002; Wiebe & Christensen, 1996). For example, the self-disciplined, diligent, and task-oriented nature of individuals scoring high on the conscientiousness trait might be associated with the most favorable adherence in patient-directed treatment contexts. In contexts where less patient control is available and the health care provider maintains extensive direction, the trusting, cooperative, and deferent style indicative of individuals high on the agreeableness dimension might be more likely to be associated with good treatment adherence.

As Kaplan and Simon (1990) have described, one approach to determining the type of treatment a particular patient is most likely to comply with is simply to ask the patient. Evidence from social psychology does suggest that some individuals are quite good at "self-predicting" the conditions under which they will behave in a certain way (Bem & Allen, 1974; Bem & Funder, 1978). Extending this idea to the medical treatment context, Kaplan and Hartwell suggest that if the important situational elements of the various regimes are described and individual patients are asked what type of regimen they are most likely to adhere to, patients' behavioral "forecasts" may be quite accurate. This possibility is certainly consistent with data from studies using more general, psychometric assessments of patient coping style or treatment preferences (e.g., Christensen et al., 1990). The possibility that idiographic or more situation-specific, self-predictions of behavior might distinguish adherent from nonadherent patients across different treatment settings is an intuitively appealing idea that deserves careful empirical attention.

Relevance to other patient populations. The utility of the interactive approach clearly is not limited to the ESRD population. For example, Dennis Turk and his colleagues have utilized a conceptually similar approach in work involving treatment outcomes among patients with chronic pain disorders (Rudy et al., 1995; Turk et al., 1998). This body of work suggests that psychological characteristics (e.g., affective distress, perceived control) are significant predictors of differential treatment response among patients with fibromyalgia syndrome and temporomandibular disorders. Among individuals with cardio-vascular disease there is evidence that certain psychological factors (e.g., a tendency to engage in maladaptive or irrational symptom appraisals) are associated with a poorer response to behavior modification–based cardiac rehabilitation programs (Christensen et al., 1999a). Although this chapter has focused on the possible interactions between patient factors and medical treatment characteristics, the next chapter will explicitly address the possibility that similar interactions exist for certain patient individual difference characteristics and the effectiveness of behavioral or psychological interventions that have been designed to enhance patient adherence.

A variety of other medical disorders have multiple treatment options that differ in terms of the role the patient takes in treatment direction or delivery. For example, the recently developed subcutaneous infusion insulin pump provides a number of potential advantages to the patient with diabetes (Marcus & Fernandez, 1996). Insulin is administered in a more continuous manner than is the case for manual insulin injections, and more immediate and specific alterations in insulin administration can be achieved. However, effective and safe use of the pump requires a high level of motivation and careful attention on the part of the patient (Marcus & Fernandez, 1996). Misuse of the insulin pump or a lack of attention to the necessary protocol (e.g., following infection control procedures, frequent blood glucose monitoring, accurate carbohydrate counting) can result in a higher risk of infection at the insulin pump insertion site, diabetic ketoacidosis, and other potential complications (Marcus & Fernandez, 1996; Reynolds, 2000). Anecdotal reports and clinical observation suggest that patients with an internal locus of control, with a high degree of trust in their health care providers, and that are motivated to take a highly active role in self-managing their diabetes do quite well with the insulin pump (Jornsay, Duckles, & Hankinson, 1988; Marcus & Fernandez, 1996). However, systematic empirical evaluation of possible patient X treatment context effects on regimen adherence or patient outcomes involving the insulin pump more generally has not yet been conducted.

Mediational considerations. One important issue still needing to be addressed involves identifying the processes that underlie (i.e., mediate) the person X context interactive patterns obtained in past research. It is not clear, for example, why an individual who prefers to a take more active, involved role in his or her own medical care would display maladaptive and potentially self-damaging nonadherence when facing a treatment context that restricts the degree of control a patient is able to exercise. Such a response seems, on the surface, to be counterproductive to the patient's goal of procuring greater personal control because nonadherence is likely to lead to poorer treatment response, a greater risk of complications and deterioration in health status, and probably a need for even closer medical supervision and more intrusive treatments. One interpretation of nonadherence in this context follows from psychological reactance theory (Brehm, 1966). As discussed in the previous chapter, patients with a strong desire for control who are undergoing a highly provider-directed dialysis treatment may attempt to reassert their perceived loss of control over their medical care by resisting instructions concerning diet, fluid intake, or other behavioral features of the treatment that they have greater control over. In other words, patient nonadherence may be one avenue for reestablishing a sense of control in an otherwise uncontrollable context.

Evidence from another study we conducted involving center hemodialysis patients provides some support for a reactance-based interpretation of nonadherence (Christensen et al., 1997a; see figure 4.5). Among patients undergoing this provider-directed form of dialysis treatment, we found that those patients possessing a more vigilant or active coping style reported significantly less perceived control over the illness and treatment context than did other patients treated with this same modality. That is, the patients high in vigilance appeared to be particularly sensitive to the limited control this form of treatment offers. Moreover, it was this lack of perceived control that largely accounted for a significant association between high vigilance and poorer patient adherence. When perceived control was statistically controlled for, the association between coping vigilance and adherence was no longer significant. This pattern of findings raises the possibility that the poor adherence observed among some patients undergoing provider-controlled medical treatments might be improved by offering the patient alternative means to exercise personal control. For example, patients might be offered the opportunity to become more involved in certain aspects of treatment decision-making (e.g., decisions about the

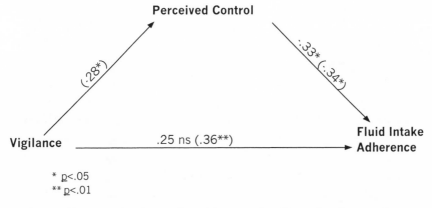

Fig. 4.5. Diagram of mediational model testing the effects of vigilance and perceived control on patient adherence. Standardized regression coefficients are reported for all paths. Coefficients outside parentheses reflect the path with the other variable controlled for in the regression analyses. Adapted from Christensen et al. (1997).

treatment schedule; input into medication selection when appropriate) even if more direct involvement in treatment delivery is not feasible.

In Conclusion

Past work suggests that medical regimen adherence might be best explained by considering the interaction of patient characteristics and treatment context factors. For example, the pattern my colleagues and I have repeatedly observed is that patients are more likely to adhere when the nature of the treatment or treatment recommendation they receive matches what they want or expect. That is, when the specific self-management demands, requirements, and degree of patient control offered by a medical treatment regimen are consistent with patients' preferences, expectations, and coping style, patients are more likely to adhere to the regimen. As intuitive as this conceptualization may be, it has rarely been applied in adherence research or in clinical practice.

Further work extending the patient X context framework to other settings, populations, and treatment regimens should underscore the utility of this framework for understanding patient treatment adherence more broadly in clinical practice. As medical technology continues to expand, the available treatment options for cardiovascular disease, diabetes, renal disease, chronic pain, and many other disorders will continue to grow as well. An increasing number of patients and practitioners will be faced with the task of selecting the treatment modality that is best suited for a particular individual and is most likely to result in adherent patient behavior and positive treatment outcome. As this occurs, it will become increasingly important that all relevant assessment information be considered when making treatment selection and implementation decisions. Attention to both patient characteristics (including psychological individual differences) and treatment context factors (e.g., the self-management demand of a particular therapy) is critical to our understanding of the types of patients that may be at risk for difficulties with adherence and the specific conditions under which these difficulties are most likely to occur.

5

Facilitating
Adherence Behavior I
Review of Techniques and Their Efficacy

Given the high prevalence and the substantial clinical and societal impact of treatment nonadherence, the design, evaluation, and implementation of interventions to improve adherence is critically important. The central objective of the present chapter is to provide a summary of the work involving interventions to improve patient adherence. In doing so, I discuss a number of important and illustrative studies in this area and highlight several key theoretical and methodological issues relevant to this body of research. These issues include a discussion of how future adherence-intervention research can be informed and guided by the broader clinical research literature involving psychological or psychotherapeutic interventions. The chapter will also evaluate the relative utility of various adherence-enhancing strategies drawing substantially from as well as updating a previous comprehensive review of this literature (Roter et al., 1998).

The Nature of Adherence-Enhancing Interventions

Adherence-intervention strategies that have been the focus of empirical investigation have generally fallen into three broad categories: behavioral, psychoeducational, and social support based. Examples of specific strategies within each of these categories along with representative studies and citations are provided in table 5.1. Behavioral intervention likely represents the broadest category of interventions and encompasses a range of strategies targeting either the behavioral antecedents of adherence (e.g., environmental cues or social stimuli that

Table 5.1. Adherence intervention from the empirical literature.

Intervention category	Representative studies
Behavioral approaches	
Self monitoring/Medication diaries	Safren et al., 2001; Schafer et al., 1982; Wing et al., 1986
Contingency contracting	Cummings et al., 1981; Swain & Steckel, 1981; Wysocki et al., 1989
Other reinforcement strategies	Christensen et al., 2002; Grady et al., 1988; Hegel et al., 1992
Monetary incentives	Rigsby et al., 2000; Wysocki, 1989
Stimulus control	Safren et al., 2001; Christensen et al., 2002
Behavioral rehearsal/Skill building	Grey et al., 1998; Kaplan et al., 1985
Goal-setting	Christensen et al., 2002; Sallis et al., 1990
Cuing/Behavioral reminders	Finney et al., 1985; Grady et al., 1988; Rigsby, 2000
Psychoeducational approaches	
Provider or investigator-delivered education	Barth et al., 1991; Rimer et al., 1987
Written information	Sclar et al., 1991; Bertakis, 1986; Williams et al., 1986
Computer-delivered education	Edworthy & Devins, 1999
Theory-based educational approaches (e.g., Health Belief Model)	Hegel et al., 1992; Jones et al., 1987; Miller et al., 1988
Social support & social environment	
Support satisfaction/Support quality	Christensen et al., 1992; Finnegan & Suler, 1985; Catz et al., 2000
Social network size	Kaplan & Hartwell, 1987
Family environment	Christensen et al., 1992
Parental/familial communication	Davis et al., 1996

make nonadherent behavior more or less likely) or adherence-related behavioral contingencies (e.g., reinforcement of adherence-related behavior by friends or family members). As summarized in table 5.1, a range of behavioral strategies that follow from these two general principles (e.g., stimulus control, self-monitoring, behavioral contracting and positive reinforcement, behavioral rehearsal) have been examined as potentially useful tools for improving adherence.

Educational approaches include providing verbal, written, or videotaped information about an existing or potential health threat, supplying information about a treatment option, and educating patients about the costs and consequences of following a treatment regimen. Psychoeducational studies involving the modification of patients' health beliefs are also included in this category. Attempts to influence health-related beliefs have generally involved providing the patient with information about the threat of a disease or disease-related complication and the relative benefits of regimen adherence.

Finally, social support–based interventions include strategies that attempt to enhance adherence by mobilizing or enhancing existing social resources or relationships (e.g., family or relationship counseling; promoting increased social interaction) or by providing additional social support or social contact (e.g., supportive counseling, group support, supportive home visits).

Behavioral Techniques

Application to chronic treatment regimens. The utility of behavioral strategies for enhancing patient adherence has been examined for a wide variety of chronic treatment regimens. Studies in most chronic disease populations have reported modest, though inconsistent, success in applying behavioral strategies. Although not entirely consistent, in research involving individuals with hypertension, behavioral strategies (particularly those involving self-monitoring of medication dosing or home blood pressure monitoring) have generally been found effective at enhancing appointment keeping and medication adherence (Dunbar-Jacob, Dwyer, & Dunning, 1991; Edmonds et al., 1985; Haynes et al., 1976; Johnson et al., 1978). In one of the few studies directly comparing the effects of behavioral techniques with those of enhanced education, Swain and Steckel (1981) reported that patients with hypertension who had been randomly assigned to a contingency-contracting condition (i.e., setting specific adherence goals and receiving nominal rewards if goals are met) were more adherent with follow-up medical visits and displayed better blood pressure control eighteen months later than patients assigned to an enhanced-education condition. No measure of medication adherence was available in this study. The evidence linking improved adherence to improved blood pressure control in other studies is more equivocal, however (e.g., Edmonds et al., 1985).

Research involving adherence in HIV/AIDS has produced very mixed findings (Fogarty et al., 2002). In a study involving fifty-six HIV-positive individuals receiving antiretroviral medication, a simple self-monitoring intervention (a daily pill diary) yielded little improvement in adherence (Safren et al., 2001). In the same study, however, a multifaceted intervention package that included both cognitive-behavioral components (e.g., stimulus control, behavioral rehearsal, communication enhancement) and psychoeducational efforts (information provision about the disease and treatment) did produce significant improvements in adherence over a twelve-week period. Utilizing a randomized, controlled study design, Rigsby et al. (2000) examined the effects of cue-dose training on medication adherence among HIV-positive patients. Cue-dose training essentially involves helping patients to link medication dosing with personalized cues or reminders for prescribed dosing times (e.g., mealtime, tooth brushing). The study compared the potential adherence-enhancing effect of three conditions: cue-dose training alone, cue-dose training with the addition of monetary incentives for adherent behavior (up to $280 over four weeks), and a control group that received nondirective but encouraging feedback from study personnel. Results included an initially significant enhancement in electronically monitored medication adherence in the cue-dose training plus reinforcement condition with no improvement in the other two conditions. Even this improvement was short-lived, however, with no effect observed at an eight-week postintervention follow-up.

One of the most common applications of behavioral techniques in chronically ill populations has involved attempts to improve adherence among insulin-dependent diabetic patients (Padgett et al., 1988). A number of these studies have utilized very small n (1–5 patients) within-subject designs in attempts to demonstrate the effect of behavioral intervention techniques (e.g., Carney, Schechter, & Davis, 1983; Schafer, Glasgow, & McCaul, 1982). In one early study, Schafer et al. (1982) reported improved blood glucose monitoring among diabetic patients receiving an intervention consisting of self-monitoring, goal setting, and contingency contracting. Unfortunately, few randomized, controlled studies of the effects of behavioral intervention on diabetic regimen adherence (or adherence to medical regimens more generally) are available. A notable exception is a study by Wing et al. (1986), which observed that Type 2 diabetic patients randomly assigned to receive blood glucose self-monitoring training displayed better adherence to dietary guidelines than patients receiving usual care.

In my own research involving patients with advanced renal failure undergoing hemodialysis, my colleagues and I recently examined the efficacy of a seven-week, group-administered, behavioral self-regulation intervention designed to increase adherence to the strict fluid-intake restrictions faced by these patients (Christensen et al., 2002). An outline of the intervention program is provided in table 5.2. While we adapted the intervention to target regimen adherence among dialysis patients, the essential elements of the protocol could be adapted and applied to many other patient groups and target behaviors. The intervention program followed the general self-regulatory model outlined by Kanfer & Gaelick (1986). In earlier research, self-regulation- or self-control-based interventions had been applied to a wide range of behavioral (e.g., weight loss, smoking cessation) and emotional (e.g., depression, anxiety) problems (Kanfer & Gaelick, 1986). Self-regulation theory espouses that successfully carrying out a target behavior is a function of three core self-regulatory stages or processes including: self-monitoring, self-evaluation, and self-reinforcement of the behavior. Illustrations of these behavioral principles, group discussions, and homework assignments (e.g., practice in self-monitoring, goal-setting) were explicitly linked to the issue of fluid-intake adherence (i.e., limiting the intake of all fluids to approximately one liter per day). Twenty patients composing the intervention group were compared with twenty matched control patients on an indicator of fluid-intake adher-

Table 5.2. Summary of self-regulation protocol.

(1) Introduction and rationale for the self-regulation approach and its relation to the dialysis treatment regimen (session 1).

(2) Brief review of how and why fluid-intake guidelines are established and the immediate and long-term effects of nonadherence (session 1).

(3) An overview of the association between self-regulatory processes (i.e., self-monitoring, self-evaluation, self-reinforcement) and behavior. Examples of this overview include the effect of self-monitoring on enhancing awareness and perceived control over behavior, and the association between reinforcement contingencies and the likelihood of repeating a behavior in the future (session 2).

(4) Instruction in self-monitoring skills and begin homework self-monitoring of daily fluid intake, mood, behavior, setting, and other target behavior antecedents. A daily diary method is used with entries made each time fluid was ingested (session 3).

(5) Goal-setting discussion and patient goal-setting for fluid-intake between treatments. Homework assignment includes each patient discussing goals with his or her care providers (session 4).

(6) Establishing self-administered reinforcement strategies. Both covert reinforcers (e.g., positive self-evaluation) and overt reinforcers (e.g., engaging in pleasurable activities) are discussed. Homework assignment includes identifying realistic and adaptive reinforcers (session 5).

(7) Teaching stimulus-control, self-instruction, and related behavioral coping skills to promote regulation of fluid intake (session 6).

(8) Daily recording and evaluation of target behavior (i.e., fluid intake). Self-monitoring is reviewed and discussed during weekly group meetings (session 3–7).

(9) Weekly self-evaluation of target behavior performance and interdialytic weight gain relative to goals. Patients' use of behavioral self-regulatory coping skills also reviewed/discussed during weekly group meetings. Any problems in meeting goals are discussed (session 3–7).

ence (average interdialysis session weight gain) over an eight-week follow-up period.

Results of this study are depicted in figure 5.1 and revealed that patients in the two groups exhibited a significantly different pattern of change in fluid-intake adherence across the follow-up period. Although the intervention and control groups did not differ significantly in terms of adherence at the initial postintervention period, the two conditions did differ at the eight-week follow-up. Patients in the intervention group displayed significantly better adherence than those in

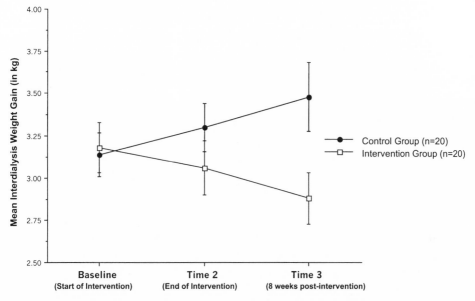

Fig. 5.1. Change in interdialysis weight gain values over time as a function of intervention status. Higher values represent poorer patient adherence with the fluid-intake regimen. From Christensen et al. (2002).

the control condition. Most other published adherence intervention research involving dialysis or renal transplantation patients (see exception by Cummings et al., 1981) has been limited to very small *n* or single-subject designs (Brantley et al., 1990; Carton & Schweitzer, 1996; Hegel et al., 1992; Hart, 1979).

The intervention package we applied in our hemodialysis patient study was broad and multifaceted, and the research design did not allow for a finer-grained examination of whether specific aspects of the intervention were particularly efficacious. I was struck, however, by the number of patients that commented on the importance of "undoing" learning that had occurred across their lifetimes and made adherence to this general type of treatment regimen more challenging. Specifically, patients participating in the intervention group often discussed the extent to which long-established patterns of eating and drinking behavior were difficult to change. As one patient put it, "all of my life I have associated food and drink with family, friends, and special times;

then one day my doctor tells me if I eat the foods I always had and drink too much fluid it could kill me, I can never get used to that." While anecdotal, this general theme may occur for any of the large number of medical treatment regimens that necessitate modification of eating or drinking behavior.

A somewhat different form of behavioral intervention that appears quite promising in select populations (e.g., adolescent patients) involves social-learning-based strategies that emphasize the role of social interaction and appropriate social skills in influencing adherence behavior (Grey et al., 1998; Kaplan, Chadwick, & Schimmel, 1985). In a study of sixty-five adolescents with Type 1 diabetes, Grey et al. (1998) randomly assigned patients receiving intensive medical management from their diabetes care providers to also receive a social-learning-based "coping skills training" intervention or to receive no such intervention. The coping component emphasized behavioral rehearsal of diabetes management skills in various social situations (e.g., managing dietary choices when eating with friends; explaining the need for medication to others). Individuals in the coping skills condition exhibited significantly better diabetic regimen adherence and more favorable diabetic control than patients in the comparison condition. This focus on social interaction and social skills is consistent with earlier theorizing concerning the importance of social norms and social influence on health behavior and may be particularly relevant to adolescents or other populations that may be particularly susceptible to peer influences (e.g., Kaplan et al., 1985). This possibility deserves further study.

In addition to the above research, behaviorally oriented strategies have proved useful for improving dietary adherence among non-insulin-dependent diabetic patients (Rabkin et al., 1983), improving medication adherence in both pediatric and adult rheumatoid arthritis patients (Nicassio & Greenberg, 2001; Rapoff, Purviance, & Lindsley, 1988), and enhancing asthma self-management in both children and adults (Creer et al., 1988; Kotses et al., 1995). The efficacy of these strategies has not been entirely consistent, however, and no specific behavioral strategy has emerged as being more useful than others.

Application to preventive regimens. The utility of using behavioral techniques to enhance adherence has been widely examined for preventive health care regimens with fairly consistent, although at times short-lived, success (e.g., Grady, Goodenow, & Borkin, 1988; King et al., 1988; Leermakers, Dunn, & Blair, 2000; McCaul, Glasgow, & O'Neill, 1992; Rosser et al., 1992). For example, Grady et al. (1988) tested the efficacy of a behavioral intervention designed to increase the frequency and regularity of breast self-examination in a sample of 153 women. Both behavioral cues or reminders and the provision of be-havior-contingent positive reinforcement (i.e., either a self-reward or an externally delivered reward for adhering to the self-examination protocol) were associated with significantly more adherent self-exami-nation behavior during the intervention period. The impact of the in-tervention appeared to be short-lived, however. After the intervention was withdrawn, breast self-examination behavior quickly returned to preintervention levels.

Daily self-monitoring of physical activity has been found effec-tive for promoting maintenance of a home-based exercise program in healthy middle-aged participants (King et al., 1988). In at least one study, improved exercise capacity as well as improved adherence has been demonstrated for healthy exercise program participants receiving instruction in self-monitoring and receiving contingent social rein-forcement for exercise (Noland, 1989). In addition to the above stud-ies, various forms of self-monitoring, stimulus control, behavioral con-tracting, and positive reinforcement have proved to be effective in reducing cardiovascular risk behaviors in healthy individuals (Sallis et al., 1990), improving dental hygiene (McCaul et al., 1992), and in pro-moting adherence to cardiac rehabilitation programs (Oldridge & Jones, 1986).

Application to acute regimens. Much less data are available involv-ing behavioral strategies to promote adherence to acute treatment reg-imens. Studies that are available have generally involved adherence to a brief (ten- or fourteen-day) antibiotic regimen (e.g., Blonna, Legos, & Burlack, 1989; Cockburn et al., 1987; Finney et al., 1985). There is little evidence to suggest that conventional behavioral strategies (e.g., self-monitoring, reinforcement, reminders) are well suited for enhancing adherence to this type of brief intervention. One noteworthy effort to demonstrate such an effect involved seventy-three young children be-ing treated with a ten-day antibiotic regimen for a middle-ear infection (Finney et al., 1985). Patients were randomly assigned to a usual care condition or to a mixed intervention consisting of instructing parents to self-monitor medication administration, an educational handout, and a telephone reminder to continue the regimen. Findings were mixed depending upon how adherence was defined. When adherence was assessed comparing the amount of liquid medication removed from the bottle with the amount that had been prescribed, adherence was better in the intervention condition. However, a urine assay of antibiotic levels revealed no advantage for the intervention condition. Moreover, clinical outcomes (resolution of the infection) did not differ between conditions.

Utilizing a somewhat different behavioral approach, Putnam and colleagues (1994) tested the effect of an intervention designed to enhance patient "commitment" to adhere among sixty adults receiving a ten-day antibiotic regimen. Patients in this study who were randomly assigned to the commitment condition provided both a verbal and written commitment to complete the regimen as prescribed by their physician. Patients in the commitment condition were also asked by the experimenters to review the efforts they had already made toward resolving their illness and were instructed to compose a plan to help them remember to take their medication. This aspect of the intervention was intended to increase the degree of subjective effort patients had invested in the goal of completing the treatment. Results demonstrated that medication adherence, assessed via unannounced pill counts, was superior for patients receiving the intervention relative to control group patients who were engaged in tasks irrelevant to the adherence issue. A similar effect was found in a pediatric sample when parents engaged in a similar brief commitment-enhancing intervention at the time medication was prescribed for their children (Kulik & Carlino, 1987).

The inherently brief nature of most acute treatments may limit the feasibility of implementation or the utility of behavioral intervention techniques that require repeated intervention contacts or a period of time for patients to assimilate behavioral skills or respond to behavioral contingencies. Briefer behavioral interventions (e.g., commitment-based interventions) may be effective in part because the essential ingredients of the intervention can be administered at a single point in time.

In sum, there is modest evidence to suggest that behavioral strategies can be effective for enhancing regimen adherence to a variety of treatment regimens. Data involving behavioral strategies appear most consistent for studies involving preventive regimens, less consistent but still quite promising for chronic treatment regimens, and somewhat more equivocal for acute treatments. Commitment-based interventions appear to be particularly well suited for enhancing adherence to short-term treatments.

More so than for any other form of adherence-enhancing intervention, behavioral intervention studies have often been limited by small sample sizes, a lack of randomization, and the absence of control or comparison conditions. Each of these methodological limitations makes the drawing of firm conclusions premature until additional, methodologically rigorous work is completed.

It is noteworthy that interventions that combine multiple behavioral strategies into an intervention package (e.g., self-monitoring plus adherence contingent reinforcement) tend to show more favorable outcomes than single behavioral techniques (e.g., self-monitoring alone). Because there are so few comparative outcome or intervention dismantling studies, however, it is difficult to draw any firm conclusions about the relative efficacy of various behavioral strategies or combinations of strategies. Finally, interventions that target ways in which social interactions might influence adherence behavior and the behavioral rehearsal of appropriate social skills may be especially effective for regimens that might be perceived as socially intrusive (e.g., extensive dietary modification) or among certain subpopulations (e.g., adolescents) that may be particularly sensitive to perceived or actual social stigma or peer judgments.

Educational Approaches

At a general level, educational strategies have garnered more attention as potential agents of change in patient adherence behavior than any other type of intervention. Providing patients information about their disease and prescribed treatment regimen has long been considered a fundamental component of ethical and efficacious patient care. Research and practice in many health-related disciplines (medicine, public health, nursing, dietetics, social work, and psychology, to name a few) have often asserted that patient health education is of central importance to behavior change and improved health. Moreover, as discussed in chapter 3, the role of patient education is central to some of the most influential theories of health behavior and adherence. For example, the Health Belief Model (Rosenstock, 1966) asserts that patients are most likely to adhere to a treatment regimen when the perceived threat of disease or disease-related complications is high and when the perceived health benefits of adherence outweigh any barriers. Implicit in this formulation is the notion that adherence can be enhanced by providing patients with information concerning the threat posed by a current or potential future disease and the relative benefits of regimen adherence in terms of reducing that threat.

Application to chronic treatment regimens. Research involving the effect of educational or information-based interventions on patient adherence has been a common focus of research attention but has produced mixed results. The most compelling data regarding the adherence-enhancing effect of patient education have come from studies involving patients with chronic conditions. Noteworthy studies have examined adherence in hypertension (Levine et al., 1979; Morisky et al., 1980), arthritis (Edworthy & Devins, 1999), insulin-dependent and non-insulin-dependent diabetes (Barth et al., 1991; de Weerdt, Visser, Kok, de Weerdt, & van der Veen, 1990), congestive heart failure (Rich et al., 1996), asthma (Gallefoss & Bakke, 1999), and psychiatric disorders (Kelly, Scott, & Mamon, 1990). For example, in a multicenter study involving 558 individuals with Type 1 diabetes, an educational intervention involving four one-hour sessions focusing on basic information about the pathophysiology of diabetes, the importance of diet, insulin and blood glucose monitoring technique, and diabetes-related complications was associated with significantly enhanced, self-reported adherence to the patients' insulin management and blood glucose monitoring regimen (de Weerdt et al., 1990). Similarly, in a study of sixty-two individuals with Type 2 diabetes, an intensive nine-hour intervention was associated with enhanced self-care and adherence (Barth et al., 1991).

Efficacious educational interventions in diabetes have typically consisted of multiple hours of specific information about diabetic illness and the diabetic treatment regimen. In other populations a significant adherence-enhancing effect has been obtained for much more circumscribed educational efforts as well (e.g., Sclar et al., 1991; Levine et al., 1979; Rimer et al., 1987). Cancer patients randomly assigned to receive a brief fifteen-minute "nurse education" session reported greater pain medication adherence one month later relative to patients in a control condition (Rimer et al., 1987). Similarly, a fifteen-minute educational session focusing on a review of the medication prescribed and the dosing instructions was associated with significantly improved medication adherence and improved appointment keeping (Levine et al., 1979). Sclar al. (1991) reported that hypertensive patients receiving a monthly educational newsletter and periodic brief telephone contact demonstrated more favorable adherence.

One recent study examined the utility of computer-delivered patient education for enhancing medication adherence among osteoarthritis patients (Edworthy & Devins, 1999). Patients randomized to the intervention condition interacted with a thirty-minute computer program providing information about their disease, medication effects and side effects, patient involvement in treatment-related decision-making, and communication with health care providers. The intervention was associated with improved medication adherence over an eight-week follow-up period. This study is particularly noteworthy because the authors attempted to identify mediators of the effect of their intervention on adherence. Evidence suggested that improved medication adherence observed in the computer-administered education condition was, in part, mediated by increased self-efficacy, perceived ease of adherence, and more accurate expectations of drug effects.

Even though some intervention studies involving chronic conditions have reported that education-based protocols are associated with improved adherence, the data are not consistent. A number of other studies involving similar intervention strategies and many of the same patient populations (chronic obstructive pulmonary disease, psychiatric disorders, cardiovascular disease, asthma, Type 2 diabetes, hypertension) have failed to find an adherence-enhancing effect for patient education (Devine & Pearcy, 1996; Elixhauser et al., 1990; Maiman et al., 1979; Miller et al., 1988; de Weerdt, Visser, Kok, de Weerdt, & van der Veen, 1991; Webb, 1980). In one noteworthy study, 123 African

American patients with hypertension were randomly assigned to a patient-education, supportive-counseling, or usual-care condition (Webb, 1980). A nurse health educator provided the educational intervention in three one-hour group sessions. Intervention sessions focused on the causes and implications of hypertension, the importance of dietary changes and regular exercise, and specific information about medication effects (both intended benefits and potential side effects). Results indicated that neither education nor supportive counseling improved medication adherence, appointment keeping, or blood pressure control.

Application to preventive regimens. Considerable attention has been focused on the effectiveness of educational approaches for enhancing adherence to preventive regimens. A range of recommended or prescribed preventive regimens have been considered including immunizations, mammography, and other forms of medical risk factor screening, physical activity programs, dietary change, and smoking prevention or cessation (e.g., Herman, Speroff, & Cebul, 1994; Karvetti, 1981; Lerman et al., 1992; Levine, 1982; McAuley et al., 1994; Taylor, Houston-Miller, Killen, & DeBusk, 1990). The outcome data for primary prevention interventions clearly are more equivocal than for studies involving patients with established disease. Many studies involving preventive regimens have reported either no effect (e.g., Herman, Speroff, & Cebul, 1994; van der Bij, Laurant, & Wensing, 2002) or a very modest effect (Burke, Dunbar-Jacob, & Hill, 1997; Lerman et al., 1992; Levine, 1982) on adherence. Conclusions reached in more comprehensive literature reviews of specific types of preventive regimens generally mirror this rather pessimistic evaluation of the broader prevention literature. For example, in a review of the effectiveness of thirty-eight studies involving physical activity interventions in older adults there was little evidence that education alone enhanced patient adherence (van der Bij et al., 2002). Effects that were identified tended to be modest and short-lived. A similarly pessimistic conclusion about the utility of educational approaches was reached in a review of forty-six studies involving adherence with prescribed or recommended cardiovascular disease prevention strategies (e.g., exercise, dietary change, smoking cessation) (Burke et al., 1997).

Application to pediatric regimens. As discussed in chapter 1, nonadherence among pediatric patients is particularly high. The limited available data involving any adherence-enhancing effects of education efforts directed toward the parents of pediatric patients (or less often, towards the patients themselves) are quite discouraging (e.g., Bertakis, 1986; Zahr, Yazigi, & Armenian, 1989). A brief informational session concerning the child's susceptibility to complications, severity of the disease, and benefits of the treatment regimen provided along with related written material failed to enhance medication adherence among young children being treated for acute ear infections (Bertakis, 1986). A similar nurse-administered educational intervention had no significant effect on adherence to dietary recommendations or appointment keeping among parents of infants being seen in a "well-baby clinic" (Zahr et al., 1989).

Williams and colleagues (1986) conducted one of the few education-based studies that reported successfully enhancing adherence to an acute pediatric medication regimen. This study actually used a combination of verbal and written information along with behavioral cues (reminder stickers) and a medication monitoring system. Although results were encouraging, it was impossible to determine the relative importance of the information provided to parents versus the behavioral component of the intervention. In general, identifying strategies effective for enhancing adherence to pediatric regimens is a relatively neglected area of adherence research with few promising findings to date but with very important implications for patient outcomes.

In sum, the available evidence for educational approaches to adherence enhancement is modest and varies across different populations and treatment regimens. The strongest evidence exists for chronic treatment regimens, particularly those involving medication treatments for hypertension. The evidence for preventive regimens is more equivocal. Published studies involving acute treatments or pediatric regimens are too limited to draw even preliminary conclusions.

Few factors have been identified that might distinguish efficacious from nonefficacious educational interventions. The studies described above suggest that more-specific or more highly targeted educational efforts (e.g., Barth et al., 1991) seem superior to more-general or broader health education (e.g., Hawe & Higgins, 1990). Multifaceted or more complex treatment regimens (e.g., diabetic regimen, renal dialysis regimen) appear to require more intensive educational efforts than single-faceted or less-complex treatments (e.g., antihypertensive treatment, acute medication regimens). Potentially different effects as a function of the type of provider or educator that delivers the intervention have not been explicitly examined. However, the available studies suggest that pharmacist-delivered education is relatively less effective (e.g., Berger et al., 1991; Hawe & Higgins, 1990) than is education delivered by a nurse or health educator.

Although most studies have involved educational material being presented verbally and "face to face" to the patient, there are insufficient data to conclude that this more costly mode of information delivery is superior to written, videotaped, or computer-administered education. Finally, some studies (e.g., Bertakis, 1986; Hegel et al., 1992; Jones, Jones, & Katz, 1987; Miller et al., 1988) have designed educational interventions that parallel the specific components of the Health Belief Model (focusing on perceived threat of disease or complications and the benefits of and barriers to adherence) or the Theory of Reasoned Action (focusing on patient attitudes and perceived social norms). However, there is no clear evidence that these theoretically based interventions are superior to the more-general or ad-hoc provision of treatment and disease-related information.

Two particularly important methodologic problems are present in the available education-focused adherence studies. First, the vast majority of intervention studies across all treatment regimens have relied on patient self-reports as a measure of adherence (e.g., Barth et al., 1991; Hawe & Higgins, 1990; Miller et al., 1988; Rimer et al., 1987; Williams et al., 1986). Studies not relying on subjective self-reports have often utilized similarly limited, indirect assessments like pill counts or pharmacy refill records (e.g., Sclar et al., 1991; Edworthy & Devins, 1999). Although adherence researchers have made considerable strides in refining the assessment of adherence behavior (see chapter 1 for an extended discussion of this issue), these advancements have, for some reason, generally failed to be incorporated into adherence intervention studies. One might speculate that given the typically more intensive efforts required to design and conduct an intervention study, intervention researchers are reluctant to devote still more effort and additional cost to incorporate adherence assessment methodologies that do not rely on self-report (e.g., electronic monitoring, biological assays). This is unfortunate given the critical importance of obtaining valid and reliable adherence assessments. Additional attention to adherence outcome assessment in this area of research would be time and money well spent.

A second common methodological problem in adherence intervention research has involved the fact that many interventions ostensibly designed to test the specific effect of education on adherence are actually quite nonspecific, as they involve a mix of education and other intervention strategies. Most commonly, educational intervention is confounded with one or more behavioral intervention strategies (e.g., Blonna, Legos, & Burlack, 1989; Hatcher et al., 1986; Williams et al., 1986). In other cases the provision of education occurred within the context of a supportive counseling intervention or substantially enhanced contact with providers, making it difficult to determine whether the educational material itself had an effect on adherence that was independent of increased attention, support, or other "non-specific effects" (e.g., Bailey et al., 1990; Rich et al., 1996). Evaluating the specific effect of patient education is central to drawing any conclusions about the utility of this approach relative to other strategies for enhancing adherence. It is also central to drawing more general conclusions about the utility of health belief or health education–based models of behavior change.

Social Support-Based Approaches

As discussed in chapter 2, considerable evidence in a range of medical populations suggests that the availability and perceived quality of social support are important correlates of regimen adherence. In contrast to the large number of observational or descriptive studies involving social support and adherence (discussed in chapter 2), few adherence studies have been published that involve the experimental manipulation or attempted enhancement of social support. In general, the reported findings are fairly discouraging. For example, a meta-analytic review of the effect of psychosocial interventions on adherence in diabetes concluded that supportive counseling or other interventions aimed at increasing social support have little effect on patient adherence (Padgett et al., 1988). This and other past literature reviews, however, have generally failed to distinguish between different types of support-based intervention (Fogarty et al., 2002; Padgett et al., 1988; Roter et al., 1998). It is possible that not explicitly distinguishing different types of supportive interventions used in various studies has obscured potential differences in the effects some interventions may have on adherence.

Increased contact with health care providers. Several categories of social support–based intervention have been empirically evaluated. The most common type of supportive intervention described in the adherence literature involves providing patients increased contact with a health care provider or with study personnel (e.g., Garrity & Garrity, 1985; Kirscht, Kirscht, & Rosenstock, 1981; Weinberger et al., 1991). These studies suggest that increased contact with providers is beneficial in terms of patient adherence, but the effects vary substantially according to how and where the support is provided. For example, in a review of the results of four studies involving adherence to antihypertensive medication regimens, supportive home visits by members of the health care team seemed to be associated with a more consistent pattern of enhanced adherence than did support provided to patients during a clinic visit (Garrity & Garrity, 1985). In a study involving four hundred patients being treated for hypertension, supportive contact with a health care provider and with an existing friend or family member was combined (Kirscht et al., 1981). A study nurse visited patients in their homes on a single occasion to offer emotional support and to discuss problems encountered in following the treatment. The nurse also met with a support person who had been identified by the patient and encouraged that individual to maintain contact with the patient and to provide support. This intervention was associated with a significant enhancement in medication adherence according to both patient self-reports and pharmacy records. A study involving medication adherence among adolescents explicitly compared the effects of support provided by a "peer counselor" and support provided by a "nurse counselor" (Jay et al., 1984). The peer-based support proved most effective at enhancing adherence over a four-month period.

Patient support groups. Another type of support-based intervention involves participation in a patient support group. Although the existence of various types of patient support groups has become ubiquitous for many patient populations, rigorous data regarding the effects of support group participation have proved hard to come by. This is particularly true in the case of regimen adherence. The limited data that are available regarding the effect of patient support groups on adherence is mixed (e.g., Nessman, Carnahan, and Nugent, 1980; Robison, 1993; Van Es et al., 2001; Wysocki et al., 2000). In one early study patients being treated for hypertension were randomly assigned to an eight-week patient support group facilitated by a nurse and a psychologist, or to an eight-week education-only condition (education was delivered via audiotape) (Nessman, Carnahan, & Nugent, 1980). Relative to patients in the education-only condition, patients participating in the weekly support group exhibited more favorable medication adherence (determined by pill counts) and better clinic attendance records. However, in a study of 112 adolescents being treated for asthma, a very different pattern was obtained (Van Es et al., 2001). A supportive intervention consisting of three ninety-minute, nurse-led patient support groups and four individual supportive counseling sessions with a nurse failed to increase adherence to inhaled prophylactic asthma medication. Similarly, participation in ten weekly support group sessions led by a nurse and health educator had little effect on adherence among individuals with insulin-dependent diabetes (Wysocki et al., 2000). The support group outcome findings are clearly limited and equivocal at this time.

Enhancing familial support. A different type of socioemotional approach to enhancing adherence involves interventions aimed at increasing the supportiveness of a patient's current family or social environment (Morisky et al., 1985; Wysocki et al., 2000). In one such study, patients with hypertension were randomly assigned to receive a single-session family counseling intervention focusing on enhancing expressions of support within the family and increasing the degree to which family members show support for the patient's efforts to comply with treatment (Morisky et al., 1985). Patients in the family support condition exhibited better self-reported medication adherence, better attendance at follow-up appointments, and better blood pressure control than patients assigned to a control condition.

Many studies of attempts to increase family support or influence familial relationships as a way of enhancing adherence have involved poorly described interventions lacking structure or any underlying theoretical framework (e.g., Galatzer et al., 1982; Morisky et al., 1985). An exception is a study by Wysocki and colleagues (2000) examining the effect of Behavioral Family Systems Therapy (BFST: Robin and Foster, 1989) on adherence in adolescent diabetic patients. BFST targets several aspects of family functioning, including familial problem solving, communication skills, and systemic characteristics of the family that may impede communication or problem solving. Contrary to expectation, the BFST intervention had no significant effect on self-reported diabetes regimen adherence. Objectively determined adherence data (a measure of blood glucose control) were also obtained. Interestingly, male patients whose families participated in the intervention exhibited improved blood glucose control over a three-month follow-up period. However, female patients whose families participated actually showed poorer diabetic control over time. Although the intervention procedure was well described, several methodologic shortcomings (e.g., baseline differences between study conditions) limited the ability of the authors to draw conclusions about the utility (or seeming limited utility among female patients) of this intervention program.

In sum, the focus in this section has been on studies that examined highly specific or relatively homogeneous support-based interventions. In other adherence studies the social support component of the intervention has been confounded with patient education, behavioral strategies, or some other type of psychosocial intervention, making it difficult to determine the unique effect of the support component (e.g., Bailey et al., 1990; Morisky et al., 1985). The data that are available from the relatively "pure" examinations of support-based intervention suggest that supportive home visits by health care providers are probably the most effective form of socially supportive intervention, and support provided to patients in a clinic setting is less effective. Among adolescents, peer-based interventions and peer support appear to be more effective than support provided by health care providers. The effectiveness of support-group participation or interventions targeting the family environment as a way of enhancing adherence remain unclear and are in need of further study.

Relative to the other major categories of adherence-enhancing intervention reviewed in this chapter, data involving social support interventions are clearly in short supply. This is in contrast to the relatively large and compelling nonexperimental research literature involving social support as a correlate or predictor of adherence as well as the theoretical literature on the presumed effects of support on health-related behavior more generally (see Wills & Filer, 2001, for a review). My overall impression of the literature on social support and adherence behavior is optimistic. Social and familial characteristics and processes very likely influence adherence in important ways. More experimental research involving randomized controlled trials of supportive interventions is needed, however, to determine whether support interventions lead to the type of effects on adherence behavior that social support theorists have long predicted.

Comparative Efficacy of Adherence-Enhancing Interventions

The research published to date suggests that behavioral strategies may have the most consistent empirical support as effective tools for adherence enhancement. Multiple studies exist documenting an association between behavioral intervention and adherence to a wide range of acute, chronic, and preventive regimens. Although the data are not entirely consistent, such fundamental behavior change techniques as those involving behavioral contracting, behavioral cues, and patient self-monitoring appear to have considerable potential as strategies for adherence improvement (e.g., Swain & Steckel, 1981; Grady et al., 1988; Wing et al., 1986). In addition, compelling evidence exists that some more novel or creative behavioral applications (e.g., social skills training in adolescents; commitment-enhancing techniques for acute treatments) can be quite effective in certain situations or with certain subpopulations (Grey et al., 1998; Putnam et al., 1994).

Concluding that behavioral approaches are superior to other strategies based only on the descriptive review provided here may provide an incomplete picture of the existing research findings. First, some of the most serious methodologic limitations in this literature plague the research involving behavioral approaches. In many studies, work has been limited by small sample sizes, a lack of randomization, and the absence of control or comparison conditions. Second, there has simply been more behavioral intervention research published than for any other adherence-enhancement strategy. Although other types of strategies have less supporting evidence, there have been fewer published attempts to produce such data.

Drawing conclusions from a purely descriptive review of the adherence intervention literature about the relative effectiveness of the various types of intervention strategies is difficult. Quantitative or meta-analytic literature review offers one way to draw more useful conclusions about experimental effects than can be surmised from descriptive or simply narrative reviews. In meta-analytic review a subset of studies that meet a basic set of methodologic criteria can be identified. Statistical effect sizes between different types of interventions can then be standardized and compared after taking into account sample size differences, differences in analytic approach, and differences in the number of available studies (Rosenthal, 1991).

In the most comprehensive published meta-analytic review of adherence research to date, Roter et al. (1998) examined the results reported in 153 studies that investigated a variety of adherence-enhancing interventions. The reviewed studies involved more than twenty different medical conditions and treatment regimens. To be included in the 1998 Roter review, a study must have explicitly contrasted an adherence-intervention condition with a control condition (random assignment to condition was not a prerequisite for inclusion, however). The sample size in the study must have been ten or greater and adherence must have been quantitatively assessed (studies relying on self-reports of adherence were included). Studies published before 1977 were not included. Different intervention strategies were combined using categories similar to those described in this volume. Strategies included behavioral (e.g., self-monitoring, reinforcement of adherent behavior), psychoeducational (e.g., instruction in the reasons the treatment regimen is necessary), and affective-based or supportive (e.g., socially supportive contact or efforts to reduce emotional distress) interventions. It is important to note that the sample size required for inclusion led to the exclusion of many studies involving behavioral strategies because these studies had utilized single-subject (e.g., intrasubject replication) or small sample size designs with no control group.

According to the review by Roter and colleagues, the statistically compiled effects of each of these broad intervention categories were significantly different from the no-intervention or control conditions. Most effects ranged from small to medium in size. Somewhat larger effects were observed in studies that defined adherence using such indirect methods as prescription refill records and records of appointment making. Effects were relatively smaller for more direct assessments of medication adherence (pill counts, biochemical markers) and for actual appointment keeping (as opposed to simply appointment making). This pattern suggests that intervention effects are generally stronger when adherence is defined using measures that are further removed from actual adherence behavior. Stated differently, interventions appear to be more effective in modifying adherence intentions than in changing actual regimen adherence.

The Roter review gave some indication that adherence effects for behavioral and educational approaches were stronger than for interventions focusing solely on social support provision or on efforts to reduce patient emotional distress. There was also an indication that more comprehensive or "mixed" interventions combining cognitive, behavioral, and affective components were more effective than any of the single-focus interventions. It is difficult to know, however, if it was a particular combination of intervention strategies that was incrementally more effective or simply the fact that mixed intervention packages also typically involved more patient contact and may have differed from single-focus interventions in other nonspecific ways.

In Conclusion

The most important conclusion of the very informative review by Roter and colleagues was that no single category of intervention strategy appeared consistently stronger than any other. More recent research involving adherence-enhancing intervention strategies bears this out as well. One interpretation of this pattern is that the specific unique elements composing a particular intervention strategy are less

Table 5.3. Some general or common factors in effective adherence intervention strategies.

Increased contact between patient and provider

Increasing patient awareness that adherence will be evaluated

Repeated and explicit monitoring of adherence by patient and/or provider

Encouraging positive patient expectations for adherence improvement

Provider efforts reflect the fact that adherence is itself an important outcome

Soliciting an explicit (written or verbal) patient commitment to adhere to a specific treatment guideline

Provision of some form of reinforcement for successful adherence

important than the less specific, nonunique elements common to many or in some cases all strategies that have been systematically used to facilitate patient adherence. Many of these factors are listed in table 5.3. Such factors as increasing contact between providers and patients, making patients aware that their adherence is to be evaluated, and creating an expectation for improvement by providing patients a credible rationale for why an intervention is expected to help with treatment adherence may be very important elements for facilitating adherence behavior. Perhaps most importantly, these elements can, for the most part, be broadly applied without highly specialized provider or patient training.

The lack of any clear advantage for a particular strategy or approach must not be construed as equivocating the importance of intervention efforts in general. To the contrary, the available evidence clearly demonstrates that structured interventions delivered by health care providers or adherence investigators and aimed at enhancing patient adherence do produce behavior change and are obviously superior to doing nothing. The question that remains is, which intervention approach might be most effective under what conditions or for what subgroup of patients? This question is one of the central issues to be addressed in the next chapter.

6

Facilitating
Adherence Behavior II

Conceptual and Methodological Issues

Even though the interest in developing interventions to facilitate patient adherence is long-standing, in many ways, the adherence intervention research literature is still in a very early stage of development. Over the past four decades, research in this area has progressed in "fits and starts," appearing to demonstrate progress in some important ways and then meeting a period of slowed progress, often in the face of an important methodological or conceptual impediment. Designing and conducting research in this area is challenging, to be sure. In addition to the many obstacles encountered in all forms of clinical intervention research, adherence intervention trials face additional challenges often inherent in conducting behavioral research in settings that are not conducive to this type of work and with clinical populations that pose unique assessment and other methodological challenges. Various environmental impediments can be present in these settings. In some medical settings it can be difficult to identify appropriate space to carry out psychologically oriented intervention. Crowded clinics or uncomfortable medical procedure rooms may not be conducive to the intervention process. Treatment schedules and the vagaries of patient flow as well as many other potential institutional barriers may also impede investigators' efforts to randomly assign patients to an intervention at a specific point in time. There is also the need for cooperation from medical staff who are usually less familiar with the objectives and needs of behavioral protocols. Moreover, the existence of a highly heterogeneous patient case-mix found in many populations and the complexity of the treatment regimens themselves all increase the number of potential study confounds that can cloud interpretation of study findings. Finally, perhaps more than in any other area of health research, adherence intervention trials typically require significant multidisciplinary collaboration at the institutional, personnel, and scientific levels.

Rather than attempt to present a detailed how-to guide for adherence intervention research, this chapter focuses on discussion of a set of conceptual and methodological themes or issues that have been largely ignored or neglected in the adherence intervention literature to date. Each of these issues will, I believe, prove to be important in shaping the utility of future adherence research.

Theory Building and "Borrowing" from the Behavioral Science and Behavioral Treatment Literature

As chapter 1 detailed, the clinical and societal significance of patient adherence behavior clearly rivals that of any other behavioral problem. Nevertheless, for some reason, patient adherence has largely failed to make the radar of most behavioral researchers and clinicians. This has long been surprising to me given the many parallels between adherence behaviors in medical populations and behavioral disorders or target problems in nonmedical populations. For example, from a learning theory perspective, adherence behavior is undoubtedly subject to the same type of antecedent influences and operant contingencies that are known to shape other types of human behavior. Unfortunately, adherence researchers have rarely drawn from broader psychological theory or the behavioral research literature when conceptualizing, designing, or conducting adherence research. This chapter begins with several examples of how broader behavioral science theory, or how findings from studies involving other behavior change targets, might be applied to the task of designing interventions to enhance patient adherence.

Behavioral control of overeating: Parallels to patient adherence. In general, adherence intervention researchers have failed to take advantage of the broader theoretical, empirical, and clinical literatures involving behavior change in other contexts and with other populations. It is almost as if adherence behavior has been viewed as so idiosyncratic that the wealth of knowledge that behavioral scientists have accumulated concerning other types of human behavior is not relevant. For example, research involving the behavioral control of overeating has resulted in the development and empirical validation of several behaviorally based intervention techniques or programs (see Wing, 2002). Clear conceptual connections exist between obesity interventions targeting eating behavior and treatment adherence behavior in many patient populations (particularly treatment regimens involving such ingestive behaviors as dietary modification or fluid restriction). Few attempts have been made, however, to draw from the literature on the behavioral control of overeating when designing or evaluating adherence-enhancing interventions. Much of the classic work in the overeating and obesity literature (e.g., Ferster, Nurnberger, & Levitt, 1962; Stuart, 1967), including research involving stimulus control, social contingencies and eating behavior, self-monitoring, and relapse prevention in dieting behavior, could provide important and relevant direction for adherence behavior research if only it were to be applied by adherence investigators.

Cognitive theory and potential cognitive intervention for adherence. Potential parallels between adherence behavior change and broader psychological theory extend beyond the more obvious connections to behavioral principles and theory. Broader research and theory involving social-cognitive processes and cognitively oriented psychological intervention may also be quite relevant to adherence behavior change. For example, several decades of work involving cognitively oriented psychological interventions (e.g., Beck et al., 1992; Beck et al., 1979; Telch et al., 1990) have shown that the identification and modification of maladaptive cognitive styles or appraisals can be effective in addressing a range of emotional or behavioral disorders and target problems (e.g., depression, anxiety, eating disorders). An analogous intervention approach might prove to be useful in enhancing treatment adherence behavior. Consistent with this possibility, the results of an early correlational adherence study published by my colleagues and me indicated that the presence of irrational or distorted health-related beliefs reported by patients with Type 1 diabetes significantly predicted treatment nonadherence (Christensen, Moran, & Wiebe, 1999). For example, patients who were prone to making overgeneralizations about health-related experiences on the basis of an irrelevant past experience (often the experience of another individual with a very different condition) exhibited poorer adherence than other patients. These data (as well as evidence involving cognitive approaches to treating many other behavioral problems) suggest that cognitive change programs directed toward the identification and modification of maladaptive, distorted thinking among individuals following a prescribed treatment regimen might be an important tool in adherence-behavior change. However, no adherence intervention studies published to date have examined the possibility that a focus on the identification and modification of potentially maladaptive cognitive appraisals might prove effective in facilitating adherence.

Control enhancement and patient adherence. Despite considerable interest in the relation of patient control beliefs to adherence, there has been little attempt to directly incorporate what is known about control-related beliefs or processes into adherence-enhancement techniques. From the perspective of research and theory regarding perceived control and adaptation to illness, one might expect that enhancing a patient's sense of control over the medical treatment process might lead to better treatment adherence (e.g., Taylor et al., 1991; Williams et al., 1998). Of course in some circumstances enhancing patient control might seem less practical than in others, as little in the way of patient control may appear objectively possible. For example, the cancer patient undergoing chemotherapy may have seemingly few opportunities to exercise control over the complex details of the chemotherapeutic regimen and may have little instrumental involvement in the actual administration of the chemotherapy. Even in cases like this, however, providing patients some degree of control over select or isolated aspects of the treatment process may lead to more favorable adaptation and adherence. For example, although patients may not be able to exert control over the administration of the treatment itself, they might be allowed to provide input into the day of the week or time of day that treatment is received, the area of the clinic in which they receive treatment, or in selecting the nurse or technician that administers it.

What some of the literature involving perceived control suggests is that even a seemingly trivial enhancement in patient control can in some circumstances facilitate adjustment or adherence (Taylor, 1983; Williams et al., 1998). Consistent with this view, in my own consultative work in medical treatment settings I have often suggested to my physician colleagues that something as simple as allowing a patient to choose to take either "one 500 milligram capsule or two 250 milligram capsules" can potentially enhance patient commitment and adherence to the regimen. A systematic controlled study of this general type of control-enhancing intervention has not to my knowledge yet been conducted. However, theory regarding control perceptions and adaptation along with suggestive data from nonexperimental work involving control and adherence suggests that strategies specifically designed to enhance patients' sense of control in the medical treatment context could prove useful in improving treatment adherence.

To date there has been a marked lack of theory guiding the development, selection, and empirical evaluation of adherence-intervention strategies. Many of the studies reviewed in this volume have, for example, evaluated what appear to be ad hoc conglomerations of intervention techniques with no clear explication of why a particular strategy or set of strategies is being evaluated in a given context. This approach seems unnecessarily limited given the wealth of knowledge pertaining to behavior change that behavioral scientists have accumulated over the years. Moreover, attention to research and theory from other areas of behavioral science may lead to potentially useful adherence-enhancement strategies not previously considered.

Patient X Intervention Interactions and Adherence Outcomes: An Alternative Conceptualization of Intervention Effects

The conclusion of essentially equivalent effectiveness among various adherence interventions mirrors the conclusion of equivalent treatment efficacy typically reached in the broader psychological treatment outcome literature (see Beutler, 1991). The so-called dodo bird verdict, that "all therapies have won, and all shall have prizes," remains a prominent view in the psychological treatment literature (Nathan & Gorman, 2002). As suggested in the previous chapter, an alternative "interactionalist" view involves the premise that certain behaviorial or psychological treatment approaches may be more likely to benefit certain subgroups of individuals. That is, individual differences in coping style, level of impairment, or degree of resistance or defensiveness might moderate psychological intervention effectiveness (Beutler, 1991). For example, Beutler and Harwood (2000) have argued that the extent to which a patient possesses an internalizing coping orientation (manifested by a shy, contemplative, emotionally controlled style) versus an externalizing coping orientation (manifested by a more impulsive, extroverted, aggressive style) has important implications for psychotherapeutic effectiveness. From this perspective, internalizing patients are expected to benefit more from a psychotherapeutic approach designed to facilitate insight and self-awareness about fears, concerns, and maladaptive behaviors, and externalizing individuals should respond more favorably to an approach directly targeting the maladaptive behaviors themselves.

In an analogous way, the utility of a given intervention intended to enhance adherence might be better understood if we consider the possibility that its usefulness varies as a function of patient characteristics or across different diseases or treatment settings. This patient X intervention technique interactive framework (see figure 6.1) suggests that patient individual differences be explicitly considered in adherence intervention research designs and that the interactions of these patient differences with the type of intervention approach being considered be formally tested. Findings from the broader psychotherapy outcome literature (Beutler and Harwood, 2000; Dance & Neufeld, 1988) and from our own descriptive adherence research (see Christensen, 2000) suggest several possible patterns of interaction between patient individual differences and adherence intervention type. For example, patients who possess characteristically more active or externalizing styles of coping with illness or treatment-related issues may garner more benefit from intervention strategies that are more patient directed or self-managed (e.g., self-monitoring, self-reinforcement) or

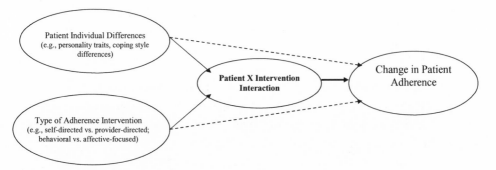

Fig. 6.1. Conceptual representation of the interactive framework applied to adherence intervention research.

that are more instrumental in focus (e.g., behavioral skill building, behavioral rehearsal). In contrast, a more directive or provider-controlled approach to enhancing adherence (e.g., behavioral contracting, external inducements, provider instruction or direction) or a more affective-focused approach (e.g., supportive counseling) may be most likely to benefit patients with more passive, avoidant, or internalizing styles.

Many other individual difference characterizations are also potentially relevant and important to consider. For example, the potential importance of the Five-Factor Model of personality as an organizing framework for patient assessment (see chapter 3) has been highlighted in both the adherence (Wiebe & Christensen, 1996) and psychotherapy literatures (Anderson, 1998). Patients high in trait conscientiousness (who are characteristically more self-reliant) might be expected to benefit most from interventions offering or requiring greater patient involvement and direction. Patients high in neuroticism (who have a strong tendency to experience chronic, dysphoric emotions) may garner particular benefit from affective-based interventions designed to reduce emotional distress. Patients high on the agreeableness dimension (who are characteristically more trusting and more deferent to others) may respond better to group-based or interpersonally oriented strategies, and those low in agreeableness may be relatively more likely to benefit from individual-based or less confrontive approaches.

Few of the adherence-related studies conducted to date have considered the possibility that the efficacy of a given intervention approach may be more effective for certain subgroups of patients. If such patient X intervention-type interactions do exist, simply comparing the strength of the main effects that various interventions have on adherence without consideration of patient factors is wholly insufficient. This possibility is important for adherence researchers to explore. The end goal of such efforts is determining what type of intervention approach is most effective for what type of individual patient under what illness or treatment-related circumstances.

Methodological Challenges and Direction for Future Intervention Research

Many of the most important methodological limitations present in adherence intervention research have been highlighted in the previous chapter. Here I will extend this discussion and highlight other methodological issues that have received limited attention by adherence researchers but that seem essential for future research to consider.

The search for experimental control. The lack of experimental control is certainly one of the most important limitations of this area of research. Studies lacking control groups, devoid of random assignment, and with very small sample sizes abound, and each of these limitations can cloud interpretations of intervention effects. Without an appropriate control group it can be difficult or impossible to determine whether apparent intervention effects are due to the intervention itself or would have occurred even without the intervention. However, it is important to recognize that adherence researchers may face circumstances or situational constraints that preclude random assignment or the degree of experimental control that may be possible in other clinical research contexts. For example, investigators may not be able to assign patients from different medical clinics to the same experimental protocol at the same time due to institutional or other constraints. In cases like this, both within-subject research designs and quasi-experimental, between-subject research designs can play an important role in demonstrating the relevance or efficacy of a given form of intervention in facilitating patient adherence.

In within-subject designs, individual patients serve as their own controls as an intervention is applied and removed (or a different intervention is substituted) at discrete times and commensurate changes in behavior are recorded. For example, Hegel and colleagues (1992) utilized a multiple-baseline design to evaluate the effects of a cognitive-behavioral adherence intervention package. Various components of the intervention were introduced and then removed across a two-month period with commensurate changes in patient adherence recorded. This strategy allowed the investigators to identify a short-term adherence effect for an intervention strategy targeting patient health beliefs and a more sustained improvement in adherence after the introduction of positive reinforcement for adherent behavior.

In quasi-experimental research designs patients are not randomly assigned to intervention conditions; rather, preexisting groups of individuals are generally compared, with one group receiving a given intervention and the other group serving as a control or comparison condition. In some cases, matching of patients composing the different groups is done to minimize group differences on key characteristics. Matching can be one particularly useful way for investigators to buttress a quasi-experimental design, building a stronger case for the interpretation of treatment effects when patient randomization was not implemented. For example, in one of our recent studies involving adherence among hemodialysis patients, those patients receiving a behavioral intervention were matched with non-randomly assigned control group patients from a different dialysis clinic on several variables (e.g., age, gender, disease severity, baseline adherence) demonstrated in previous work to be associated with adherence in this population (Christensen et al., 2002a). Through a combination of using a non-randomly assigned, no-treatment control group, and with additional steps taken to minimize potential between-group differences, some, but not all, of the potential threats to study validity were minimized. For example, it was unlikely that seasonal changes in adherence differed between the various study centers or that regression to mean explained the improvement in adherence seen in the intervention condition.

Both within-subject and quasi-experimental research designs can play an important role in helping to demonstrate empirical support for an adherence intervention technique. These research designs can also be very useful in helping investigators decide if a particular adherence intervention approach is worth pursuing using a more rigorous and costly approach. When feasible, however, fully randomized, prospective clinical trials reflect the gold standard evaluative strategy in adherence intervention research and allow for the most definitive interpretation of study effects and offer the greatest control over threats to study validity.

Demonstrating clinical significance in adherence intervention research. In the broader psychological intervention literature, the importance of considering the extent to which treatment effects are clinically meaningful, in addition to being statistically significant, is becoming increasingly clear (Kendall, 1999). Although the issue of clinical significance seems equally important in the case of adherence behavior, few adherence intervention studies have considered the clinical significance of intervention effects. Various strategies for demonstrating clinical significance have been articulated in the broader literature (Jacobson et al., 1999; Kendall et al., 1999). One commonly espoused approach involves making comparisons between treated individuals and normative data, that is, evaluating the extent to which individuals undergoing a given intervention return to the normative or "nondysfunctional" range of functioning (typically within two standard deviations of the population mean) on a clinically relevant outcome variable (Jacobson et al., 1999). For example, a treatment study of depression could make comparisons between level of depression in a treatment group and normative data about depression level in nondepressed samples. However, such comparisons can be difficult in the context of adherence research. Normative information about adherence behavior is scarce and is rarely generalizable from one clinical population to another or to the general population or other normative samples. Moreover, in many cases nonadherence is actually statistically normative for a given patient population (i.e., greater than half of the target population may be nonadherent according to clinical guidelines) making statistical comparisons with the "normative" range of patient behavior largely meaningless. On the other hand, comparing adherence levels in an intervention group to a clinical criterion or standard reflecting "good adherence" may be overly conservative and minimize the importance of meaningful improvements in adherence that do not reach an aspirational, often arbitrary, clinical standard.

The most useful methods of evaluating clinical significance in adherence research may be less direct than in other domains of behavioral intervention research. Such evaluations should involve a consideration of the extent to which a change in adherence is associated with a commensurate change in a related clinical or health outcome. For example, a researcher might explicitly evaluate whether the change in adherence observed in a study of medication adherence among individuals with hypertension is associated with a clinically meaningful change in blood pressure or whether the change in adherence observed in a study of individuals with diabetes is associated with a clinically significant change in blood glucose levels. Using a clinical or health outcome as a criterion can lead to very different (and probably more useful) conclusions about the clinical significance of an intervention effect than one would reach attempting to make normative comparisons of the adherence behavior itself.

As an illustrative example of using data concerning health-related changes to evaluate the significance of changes in adherence behavior, consider a hypothetical study of a technique to promote adherence to an antihypertensive medication regimen. At baseline, average adherence to the regimen (as determined by the proportion of pills taken versus the number prescribed) is 50 percent for both control and intervention condition patients. After the intervention is administered, average adherence in the intervention condition is 65 percent and remains at 50 percent in the control condition. From a normative comparison perspective, the investigator might conclude that although medication adherence improved by 30 percent, the intervention was not clinically significant because the intervention group remained in the nonadherent range (with 35 percent of prescribed pills still not being taken by the patient). However, if the investigator finds that this incremental improvement in medication adherence was associated with a 30 percent improvement in blood pressure, the intervention effect may very well be deemed to be clinically meaningful. From this perspective, the parallel gathering of information concerning changes in health as well in the adherence behavior itself is an important part of determining the clinical significance of adherence intervention effects.

Study efficacy vs. intervention effectiveness. Another important set of issues involving adherence intervention research is the translation of findings from controlled intervention efficacy studies to the actual ef-

fectiveness of an intervention in the "real world" of patient management. The relation between the efficacy and effectiveness of treatment
outcomes is an increasingly important consideration in both medicine
and behavioral science (Lipsey & Wilson, 1993; Nathan, Stuart, &
Dolan, 2000). The majority of intervention studies reviewed in the
previous chapter involved efforts to demonstrate intervention efficacy
under controlled experimental conditions. The extent to which the
outcomes reported in efficacy studies parallel the general effectiveness
that these same interventions are likely to have with more heterogeneous patient groups in more diverse, real-world settings is less clear
and requires careful consideration.

    In the published research involving the effectiveness of adher-
ence-enhancing interventions, several issues are particularly important
to consider. First, patients making up the study samples in adherence
research may, due to patient self-selection, differ in composition from
the broader treatment population under consideration. Although sample generalizability is a challenge in all treatment outcome research, a
particular problem in adherence research involves the fact that the behavior of interest (patient adherence) is likely to be confounded with
the willingness of patients to participate in a research trial and to comply with the requirements of a study protocol. In other words, the least
adherent patients (who may be most in need of intervention in the
"real world") are very likely to be underrepresented in adherence-effi-
cacy study samples. A related issue involves the level of motivation patients are likely to have to participate in an intervention that may require considerable effort or commitment. Unlike patients presenting
for treatment for most psychological or medical problems, nonadherent patients are much less likely to be subjectively distressed by their
behavior. This lack of distress may impede the efficacy of a study intervention and limit the generalizability of study findings to the broader
patient population (which is, arguably, composed of individuals who
are even less motivated to change their behavior). Finally, the resources
or personnel necessary for the effective implementation of adherence
interventions are likely limited in many medical settings. Recognition
is rapidly growing that patient nonadherence poses a significant threat
to contemporary medical care. However, even in the presence of compelling data indicating that adherence-enhancing interventions are po-

tentially effective, many health care settings may not currently have the dedicated resources available to implement the indicated interventions. Demonstrating the applicability and effectiveness of adherence intervention programs is possible but will require sustained attention from adherence researchers and clinicians, medical care providers, and health care systems.

Toward empirically supported adherence interventions. The standardization and empirical validation of specific interventions for specific psychiatric and behavioral disorders has emerged as an important goal in the mental health treatment literature (see Nathan & Gorman, 2002). Standardizing interventions allows for methodological replication across research studies and domains and, ultimately, allows for more feasible and reliable implementation in clinical settings. Moreover, by focusing on the empirical validation of specific interventions for specific treatment populations, the confidence that practitioners, patients, and policy makers have in the intervention strategies is likely to be increased. Adherence intervention research has lagged behind the medical and mental health treatment literature in demonstrating empirical support for specific intervention programs for specific clinical populations or treatment regimens. Relatively little effort has been made to standardize and empirically validate adherence intervention programs so that the programs can be reliably transported and reproduced by other investigators. A move toward greater specification and standardization of adherence intervention protocols is needed and will allow for more precise replication of efficacy research by multiple investigative teams. This type of replication, as well as greater attention to real-world effectiveness trials, is needed to raise adherence intervention research and practice to par with other types of behavioral and mental health treatment programs.

In Conclusion

Despite the efforts of adherence researchers over the past several decades to formulate and validate empirically supported and clinically effective adherence intervention programs, considerable work remains ahead. Methodologic shortcomings must be addressed, and researchers must broaden their thinking about the types of interventions that might be useful in facilitating adherence and begin to explicitly consider factors that might influence or moderate intervention effectiveness. Moreover, without change in the attitudes and priorities of medical care providers and health care systems, adherence researchers and clinicians will continue to be handicapped in their efforts. Medical care must move beyond simply recognizing patient nonadherence as a nuisance to recognizing it as a clinical phenomenon worthy of attention and of treatment in its own right. Contemporary health care must progress to a state where the connection between the medically indicated treatment of a disorder and the explicit facilitation of patient adherence to the treatment is seamless, even synonymous. The burden of the nonadherence epidemic is now clear, and the potential of adherence-enhancing interventions for decreasing this burden is becoming increasingly clear. Without a significant share of health care resources and health care provider attention being devoted to improving patient adherence, however, this potential will not likely be realized.

7

Bridging the Gap
Challenges for Behavioral Science
and Biomedicine

The latter part of the twentieth century witnessed unprecedented technological advances in biomedicine, yet there continued to be one constant. Human behavior change remained a necessary condition, the linchpin, really, of virtually every form of modern medical intervention. Regardless of the potential efficacy of the modern physician's armamentarium, if a patient does not present to the appropriate clinic at the appropriate time, the treatment process cannot begin. If a patient does not fill the prescription written by the provider, the treatment process cannot proceed. If a patient does not take the medication as directed, harm to both that patient and future patients may occur. If a patient does not engage in appropriate self-care after medical or surgical intervention, potential healing may never be realized.

Research involving patient adherence is now at a crucial crossroads. Evidence for the prevalence and significance of nonadherent patient behavior is now undeniable. As chapter 1 described, between 20 and 80 percent of patients do not adhere to the basic requirements of their medical treatment regimen, and patient nonadherence is associated with an estimated $100 billion annually in economic costs as well as an untold toll in patient morbidity and increased mortality (Berg et al., 1993; Dunbar-Jacob & Schlenk, 2001). In past decades, medical care providers have been slow or reluctant to recognize the fact that a great number of their treatment prescriptions or recommendations would never be carried out. This reluctance seems to be diminishing. A gradual but steady increase in adherence-related research in medical journals, and increased discussion at professional meetings, and in clinical settings, suggests that awareness of this issue among medical professionals may be increasing (e.g., Trostle, 1997).

Although recognition of the significance of nonadherence seems to be on the increase, attempts to address the problem in the "trenches" of health care delivery have lagged behind. As chapter 5 detailed, a number of intervention approaches (or combinations of approaches) have received at least modest empirical support as efficacious strategies for facilitating adherence behavior in a variety of clinical populations and settings. However, the translation of that research into effective clinical practice has generally been slow to develop. In most health care settings, even if providers recognize patient nonadherence as a problem, this recognition is still often met with resignation that treatment nonadherence is an unfortunate but immutable source of error in the health care delivery process that must simply be tolerated or is not the health care provider's responsibility to address.

Extending the Medical Model: Behavior as the Linchpin

Two fundamental shifts in thinking are necessary for moving adherence research and practice to a point where a broad-based substantive impact on treatment outcomes can be made. The most obvious paradigmatic shift involves the need for medical care providers and for health care systems to recognize adherence behavior as a necessary condition for the effective delivery of health care. The fact that behavioral processes remain largely absent, despite all of the evidence of their relevance, from the radar screen of contemporary medicine is troubling to many behavioral health scientists and has certainly impeded the impact that research and knowledge about adherence behavior has had on clinical practice and outcomes. This lack of attention can be seen in medical training programs across the country where attention to adherence or other behavioral processes in medical curricula remains scant. This absence of attention to adherence-related issues is also evident at the primary health-related research funding agencies. At the National Institutes of Health, adherence-based research funding remains relatively limited. At the National Institute of Mental Health, the fostering of adherence-related research has recently been named a priority. Still, in fiscal year 2001 only about 1 percent ($12 million) of the $1.1 billion NIMH budget funded research with a central objective of examining predictors of adherence or adherence-related interventions (Timothy Cuerdon, personal communication). The degree of adherence research funding is considerably less at other NIH institutes.

Considered within the history and context of the dominant medical paradigm, this lack of attention to behavioral issues in general, and the issue of adherence in particular is not really surprising. The traditional biomedical model has been the bedrock of medical training, science, and practice for well over a century (Engel, 1977). The biomedical model is explicitly *reductionistic* in its conception of disease etiology and is *mechanistic* in its view of the treatment of disease (see figure 7.1). A central directive of the model is to attempt to reduce a patient's physical complaints or disorder to as fundamental of a pathophysiological process as possible (e.g., bacterium, gene). Once the pathogen is identified, elimination or alteration of the pathogen is presumed to result in cure. The model is reductionistic in that higher-order processes that may influence physical disease, symptoms, or treatment response (e.g., behavior, interpersonal factors, social environment) are ignored while more basic biological processes are scrutinized. The model is mechanistic in its assumption that focusing medical treatment on the correction of an isolated causal pathogen is sufficient to result in a cure. The biomedical model is also characteristically *dualistic* in that physical or biomedical processes are generally viewed as categorically distinct from, and unaffected by, mental states and processes (including behavioral factors).

There are compelling reasons that medicine has long relied on a reductionistic view of disease. For many aspects of disease management the model works. When a patient presents to the emergency de-

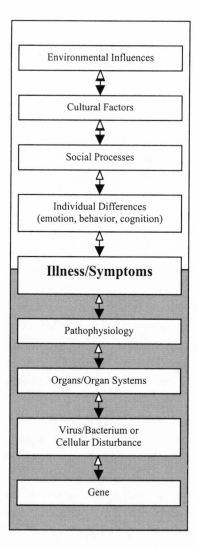

Note: Biomedical reductionism characteristically
ignores higher-order processes in diagnostic and
treatment decision making. The biopsychosocial
model assumes bidirectional causality at each level.

Fig. 7.1. Conceptual representation of the biomedical and biopsychosocial models of disease.

partment with a severed artery, isolating the fundamental pathophysiology and suturing the vessel is called for. Gaining an understanding of the patient's behavioral tendencies, emotional state, or social situation in this case seems much less germane. For an ever-increasing number of physical disorders and medical interventions, however, the traditional biomedical model clearly is insufficient. In a wide range of treatment contexts, including the management of virtually all chronic medical conditions and the treatment of many acute disorders, if the requisite patient adherence behaviors do not occur, even a complete understanding of the biomedical underpinnings of a physical disease or of the clinical pharmacology of a prescribed medication will result in an inaccurate clinical picture and an inferior treatment outcome.

Although not directly addressing the issue of patient adherence, George Engel, himself a physician, deftly illustrated the need for a new medical paradigm (Engel, 1980). Engel's proposal included arguments to adopt a "biopsychosocial model" as an alternative for medical training, science, and practice. The biopsychosocial model is based on the dynamic tenet of systems theory that processes at one systemic level are believed to reciprocally influence processes at both higher and lower levels of complexity. For example, basic pathophysiologic processes (e.g., blood pressure, viral loads, immune responses) are believed to affect and be affected by more complex intrapersonal factors and interpersonal processes (e.g., emotions, behaviors, social resources) as well as by more basic biological factors (e.g., cellular abnormalities, genetic mutations). Engel argued that an accurate and clinically astute picture of physical disease could be garnered only through a consideration of relevant processes at multiple systemic levels. Engel argued that by focusing only on lower-level physiologic processes, diagnostic and treatment decisions are incomplete and inherently error prone.

The centrality of patient adherence behavior in medical treatment fits well within this broader biopsychosocial paradigm. Any treatment plan or approach that focuses on correcting pathophysiology while ignoring individual differences in patient adherence behavior is likely to be of substantially compromised usefulness. This unfortunate scenario continues to play itself out in medical practice each time a patient leaves a clinic with a prescription in hand. From the traditional biomedical perspective, medical care delivery may end at the point the diagnosis is made and the indicated prescription or treatment plan is written by the physician. From a biopsychosocial perspective, however, treatment decision-making and delivery must also consider the attitudes, intentions, and, most importantly, the behavior of the patient after a treatment plan is formulated by the provider and after the patient leaves the clinic setting. Without this extended conceptualization of the treatment delivery process, the potential effectiveness of medical intervention protocols will continue to be significantly compromised.

Increasing evidence indicates that some domains of biomedicine are indeed beginning to recognize the utility of a biopsychosocial or biobehavioral paradigm. The past decade has, for example, seen watershed advances in understanding the reciprocal linkages between neurophysiological processes and human behavior and emotion (Davidson et al., 2002). What remains lacking, however, is any strong indication that patient behavior will soon be considered an essential component in the effective delivery of medical intervention as intuition, theory, and research evidence all indicate that it is.

Applying Behavioral Science to the Study of Patient Adherence

Although a continued shift in the way that biomedicine conceptualizes medical treatment is essential, an additional shift in perspective is necessary to bring adherence behavior to the center stage. Underscoring the lack of attention afforded behavioral processes in clinical medicine and biomedical science is critical, but may tell only half the story. Behavioral scientists and mental health professionals themselves have, in a variety of ways, contributed to the divide between behavioral and biomedical science and practice and have likely impeded the progress that has been made in addressing important behavioral issues in health care. A "reverse" mind-body dualism of sorts seems to have long plagued behavioral science and the mental health professions. As illustrated in preceding chapters, for example, behavioral and social scientists have often seemed slow to apply more general behavioral theories and concepts to the understanding of, or modification of, adherence behavior. This lack of attention might lead one to conclude from the behavioral science literature that adherence behavior must not be governed by the same fundamental principles that shape all other types of human behavior. Such a conclusion, however, would be illogical and ill-founded. In those instances when fundamental behavioral principles and techniques have been applied to the adherence issue, encouraging outcomes have usually followed.

A similar disconnect between behavioral science and adherence research appears in clinical practice contexts. For example, in my own clinical experiences over the past fifteen years in both medical and mental health settings, mental health professionals have often appeared reluctant to address the needs of patients with coexisting medical and psychological or behavioral problems because such patients are seen as overly complex or difficult to manage. Many mental health professionals seem to feel that the treatment of physically ill patients is outside their domain of practice (even when behavioral or psychological issues are the core or presenting problem). Ironically, this reluctance mirrors the attitudes of many medical practitioners who readily attend to the medical problem at hand but are reluctant to address behavioral or psychological concerns. Thus, important behavioral concerns such as patient adherence in medically ill patients are often left unattended by practitioners in both disciplines.

This marked reluctance of mental health and behavioral professionals to address patient adherence as a behavioral problem is reflected in the professional and scientific literature involving psychological treatments and psychopathology. Despite the prevalence of the problem and the costly nature of this form of maladaptive behavior, the issue has received very little attention in the broader psychological research literature on abnormal or pathological behavioral processes and disorders. For example, I recently conducted a search of the past ten years of research (1992–2001) published in *Abnormal Psychology*. *Abnormal Psychology* is arguably the leading scientific and professional journal on the etiology, assessment, and diagnosis of psychological and behavioral problems and pathologies. This search failed to reveal a single published article or study directly addressing treatment adherence behavior in any clinical population over this ten-year period. Similarly, in the leading scientific journal on the psychological treatment of psychological and behavioral problems, *Journal of Consulting and Clinical*

Psychology, a search of this same ten-year period revealed only two studies (Petry et al., 2000; Putnam et al., 1994) addressing the efficacy or effectiveness of an adherence-enhancing intervention in a medical population. Similarly, the most prominent and comprehensive texts regarding the treatment of psychological and behavioral problems and disorders have also generally failed to consider the issue of treatment nonadherence in a direct way (e.g., Bergin & Garfield, 1994; Nathan & Gorman, 2002). While a number of more specialized health psychology or behavioral health science journals (e.g., *Health Psychology; Annals of Behavioral Medicine*) commonly publish research addressing the adherence issue, the absence of attention in the broader professional or scientific literatures is glaring and seems to reflect the general reluctance of mental health professionals, psychopathologists, and psychological treatment researchers to address this issue.

Conceptualizing Nonadherence as a Behavioral Disorder

What accounts for the lack of awareness and attention that mental health professionals have afforded the issue of treatment nonadherence? One likely contributor involves the fact that patient nonadherence has never been conceptualized or formally recognized as a diagnostic entity or as a distinct form of behavioral or psychological pathology. The *Diagnostic and Statistical Manual of the Mental Disorders* (DSM-IV) greatly influences the professional perspectives as well as the research and clinical foci of many in the field. For example, treatment compendiums of empirically supported treatments are often limited to addressing disorders or problems that are formally recognized by the DSM-IV (e.g., Nathan & Gorman, 2002). According to the gold standard DSM taxonomy of behavioral and psychological disorders, "*a mental disorder is conceptualized as a clinically significant behavioral or psychological syndrome or pattern that occurs in an individual and that is associated with present distress or disability or with a significantly increased risk of suffering death, pain, disability, or an important loss of freedom*" (American Psychiatric Association, DSM-IV-TR, 2000, p. xxxi). As the literature reviewed in this volume has clearly illustrated, failure to comply with advice or instruction from a health care provider is a clinically significant phenomenon with an accompanying pattern of behavior. Such behavior is certainly associated with increased risk of death, disability, pain, and many other symptoms and complications. There is also a tremendous societal and personal cost to this disorder. Thus, although not formally recognized as a mainstream diagnostic entity in the DSM nomenclature, treatment nonadherence clearly meets this commonly accepted criteria for the definition of a behavioral or mental disorder or syndrome.

Although nonadherence is not currently recognized as a clinical disorder in the DSM-IV scheme, nonadherence to treatment is less prominently noted in the DSM-IV as a "V code"—that is, "a condition that may be a focus of clinical attention"—but is not formally recognized as distinct clinical disorder (DSM-IV-TR, 2000, p. 739). There is also an indirect reference to nonadherence contained within the DSM-IV-TR criteria for the clinical problem of "Psychological factors affecting medical condition" where a "maladaptive health behaviors" subtype is specified. Previous reports suggest that these less central classificatory categories are themselves relatively rarely used (see Stoudemire & Hales, 1995). Moreover, it is likely that the absence of a distinct DSM-IV diagnostic category, construing nonadherence as an Axis I clinical disorder, greatly reduces the salience of this issue to the many professional users of the DSM-IV. This absence also likely decreases the extent to which nonadherence is viewed as being within the purview of mental health professionals in general, many of whom might otherwise make potentially important contributions to addressing this costly behavioral problem.

Construing nonadherence as a distinct clinical disorder or syndrome would enhance the salience of this behavioral problem to practitioners, researchers, and other behavioral and mental health professionals as well as to patients, policy makers, and third-party payers. Increased awareness and recognition of the behavioral problem would likely stimulate research and funding efforts as well as efforts to address the issue in clinical practice settings. Formal recognition of this behavioral problem in the broader literature would provide an additional, highly salient forum for addressing nonadherence as a clinical concern. Finally, this form of recognition might also provide an impetus for policy makers and third-party payers to move toward recognizing the assessment and treatment of nonadherence as a directly reimbursable cost-effective clinical service. Such a move is long overdue and would certainly stimulate interest in the issue both clinically and scientifically.

In Conclusion

As those of us who work in medical contexts or with medically treated patients are keenly aware, patient nonadherence is ubiquitous in nearly all medical populations and health care contexts. The issue of patient adherence cuts across the domains of medical and behavioral science and practice more clearly than perhaps any other single issue. No other behavioral process is as inherently tied to the success of medical treatment delivery and patient outcome; no other aspect of medical care can be more clearly informed and influenced by behavioral science and practice. As I hope the material presented in this book has illustrated, there is reason to be optimistic. Important progress in addressing the adherence issue is being made. Behavioral research and theory has evolved to the point of having the potential to make substantial contributions to adherence assessment, adherence prediction, and facilitating adherence behavior. Contemporary medicine has shown signs of increasingly recognizing the importance of patient adherence behavior for treatment delivery, outcome, and evaluation.

Considerably more work is necessary, however. Progress in adherence research has been hampered by a reluctance of behavioral scientists to apply research and theory concerning behavior change more broadly, or involving other types of behaviors or behavioral disorders, to the adherence issue. Applying what is known about changing human behavior more generally to the adherence context specifically will require behavioral scientists better to educate themselves about the medical treatment context as a potential domain for their own research and practice activities. It will also require long-standing divisions in philosophy, professional turf, and training to fall. Behavioral scientists and mental health practitioners must strive to form and foster linkages with biomedical scientists and with medical practitioners. At the same time, medical professionals whose success clearly rests on the willingness and ability of patients to carry out a prescribed behavior must recognize the inherent necessity of behavioral expertise to their ability to practice effectively. Ultimately, substantive and sustainable progress in addressing this problem will require two shifts in perspective. Health care professionals must open their minds and practices to the idea that patient adherence behavior is as fundamental to the effective delivery of health care as are medical interventions themselves. Behavioral scientists must come to recognize what some of us have long believed: that the patient adherence process is as exciting, compelling, and important a context for applying and testing behavioral science and theory as one can find.

References

Ajzen, I. (1988). *Attitudes, personality, and behavior.* Chicago: Dorsey Press.

Ajzen, I., & Fishbein, M. (1980). *Understanding attitudes and predicting social behavior.* Englewood Cliffs, N.J.: Prentice-Hall.

Alagna, S. W., & Reddy, D. M. (1984). Predictors of proficient technique and successful lesion detection in breast self-examination. *Health Psychology, 3,* 113–127.

Al-Hajjaj, M. S., & Al-Khatim, I. M. (2000). High rate of non-compliance with anti-tuberculosis treatment despite a retrieval system: A call for implementation of directly observed therapy in Saudi Arabia. *The International Journal of Tuberculosis and Lung Disease, 4,* 345–349.

Alloy, L. B., & Abramson, L. Y. (1988). Depressive realism: Four theoretical perspectives. In L. B. Alloy (Ed.), *Cognitive processes in depression* (pp. 31–73). New York: Guilford Press.

Altobelli, E., Valenti, M., Verrotti, A., Masedu, F., Tiberti, S., Chiarelli, F., & Di Orio, F. (2000). Family and disease management in young type 1 diabetic patients. *Acta Diabetologica, 37,* 173–178.

American Psychiatric Association (2000). Diagnosis and statistical manual of mental disorders. Fourth edition, text revision. Washington, D.C.: American Psychiatric Association.

Ammassari, A., Murri, R., Pezzotti, P., Trotta, M. P., Ravasio, L., De Longis, P., et al. (2001). Self-reported symptoms and medication side effects influence adherence to highly active antiretroviral therapy in persons with HIV infection. *Journal of Acquired Immune Deficiency Syndromes, 15,* 445–449.

Amsel, S., Boaz, M., Ballin, A., Filk, D., Ore, N. (2002). Low compliance of iron supplementation in infancy and relation to socioeconomic status in Israel. *Pediatrics, 110,* 410–411.

Anderson, K. W. (1998). Utility of the five-factor model of personality in psychotherapy aptitude-treatment interaction research. *Psychotherapy Research, 8,* 54–70.

APPREX: MEMS Bibliography (1998). Menlo Park, Calif.: APPREX: Division of Apria Healthcare.

Apter, A. J., Reisine, S. T., Affleck, G., Barrows, E., & ZuWallack, R. L. (1998). Adherence with twice-daily dosing of inhaled steroids. Socioeconomic and health-belief differences. *American Journal of Respiratory and Critical Care Medicine, 157,* 1810–1817.

Armitage, C. J., & Conner, M. (2001). Efficacy of the theory of planned behavior: A meta-analytic review. *British Journal of Social Psychology, 40,* 471–499.

Austin, J. K. (1989). Predicting parental anticonvulsant medication compliance using the theory of reasoned action. *Journal of Pediatric Nursing, 4,* 88–95.

Bailey, W. C., Richards, J. M., Jr., Brooks, C. M., Soong, S. J., Windsor, R. A., Manzella, B. A. (1990). A randomized trial to improve self-management practices of adults with asthma. *Archives of Internal Medicine, 150,* 1664–1680.

Bame, S. I., Petersen, N., & Wray, N. P. (1993). Variation in hemodialysis patient compliance according to demographic characteristics. *Social Science and Medicine, 37,* 1035–1043.

Bandura, A. (1986). *Social foundations of thought and action: A social cognitive theory.* Englewood Cliffs, N.J.: Prentice-Hall.

Bangsberg, D. R., Hecht, F. M., Clague, H., Charlebois, E. D., Ciccarone, D., Chesney, M., & Moss, A. (2001). Provider assessment of adherence to HIV antiretroviral therapy. *Journal of Acquired Immune Deficiency Syndromes, 26,* 435–442.

Banks, W. A., Corrigan, S. A., West, J. A., Willhoit, P. P., & Ryder, P. (1996). Psychologic profiles as predictors of success in a cardiovascular risk factors life-style intervention program. *Southern Medical Journal, 89,* 971–976.

Barker, T. (1994). Role of health beliefs in patient compliance with preventive dental advice. *Community Dentristry and Oral Epidemiology, 22,* 327–330.

Barth, R., Campbell, L. V., Allen, S., Jupp, J. J., Chisholm, D. J. (1991). Intensive education improves knowledge, compliance, and foot problems in type 2 diabetes. *Diabetic Medicine, 8,* 111–117.

Basen-Engquist, K. (1992). Psychosocial predictors of "safer sex" behaviors in young adults. *AIDS Education & Preventions, 4,* 120–134.

Beck, A. T. (1967). *Cognitive therapy of depression.* New York: Guilford Press.

Beck, A. T., Rush, A. J., Shaw, B. F., & Emery, G. (1979). *Cognitive therapy of depression: A treatment manual.* New York: Guilford Press.

Beck, A. T., Sokol, L., Clark, D. A., Berchick, R., & Wright, F. (1992). A crossover study of focused cognitive therapy for panic disorder. *American Journal of Psychiatry, 149,* 778–783.

Becker, M. H., & Maiman, L. A. (1975). Sociobehavioral determinants of compliance with health and medical care recommendations. *Medical Care, 13,* 10–24.

Bem, D. J., & Allen, A. (1974). On predicting some of the people some of the time: The search for cross-situational consistencies in behavior. *Psychological Review, 81,* 506–520.

Bem, D. J., & Funder, D. C. (1978). Predicting more of the people more of the time: Assessing the personality of situations. *Psychological Review, 85,* 485–501.

Bender, B., Wamboldt, F. S., O'Connor, S. L., Rand, C., Szefler, S., Milgrom, H., & Wamboldt, M. Z. (2000). Measurement of children's asthma medication adherence by self report, mother report, canister weight, and doser CT. *Annals of Allergy, Asthma, & Immunology, 85,* 416–421.

Bensley, L. S., & Wu, R. (1991). The role of psychological reactance in drinking following prevention messages. *Journal of Applied Social Psychology, 21,* 1111–1124.

Berg, J. S., Dischler, J., Wagner, D. J., Raia, J. J., & Palmer-Shevlin, N. (1993). Medication compliance: A healthcare problem. *The Annals of Pharmacotherapy, 27,* S3–S22.

Berger, B. A., Stanton, A. L., & Felkey, B. G. (1991). Effectiveness of an educational program to teach pharmacists to counsel hypertensive patients and influence treatment adherence. *Journal of Pharmaceutical Marketing and Management, 5,* 27–37.

Bergin, A. E., & Garfield, S. L. (1994). *Handbook of psychotherapy and behavior change.* New York: Wiley.

Bergman, A. B., & Werner, R. J. (1963). Failure of children to receive penicillin by mouth. *New England Journal of Medicine, 268,* 1334–1338.

Bertakis, K. D. (1986). An application of the health belief model to patient education and compliance: acute otitis media. *Family Medicine, 18,* 347–350.

Beutler, L. E. (1991). Have all won and must have prizes? Revisiting Luborsky et al.'s verdict. *Journal of Consulting & Clinical Psychology, 59,* 226–232.

Beutler, L. E., & Harwood, T. M. (2000). *Prescriptive psychotherapy: A practical guide to systematic treatment selection.* Oxford: Oxford University Press.

Binstock, M. L., & Franklin, K. L. (1988). A comparison of compliance techniques on the control of high blood pressure. *American Journal of Hypertension, 1,* 192S–194S.

Blanc, M. H., Barnett, D. M., Gleason, R. E., Dunn, P. J., & Soeldner, J. S. (1981). Hemoglobin A1c compared with three conventional measures of diabetes control. *Diabetes Care, 4,* 349–353.

Blinder, D., Rotenberg, L., Peleg, M., & Taicher, S. (2001). Patient compliance to instructions after oral surgical procedures. *International Journal of Oral and Maxillofacial Surgery, 30,* 216–219.

Blonna, R., Legos, P., Burlack, P. (1989). The effects of an STD educational intervention on follow-up appointment keeping and medication-taking compliance. *Sexually Transmitted Diseases, 16,* 198–200.

Blumenthal, J. A., Williams, R. S., Wallace, A. G., Williams, R. B., Jr., & Needles, T. L. (1982). Physiological and psychological variables predict compliance to prescribed exercise therapy in patients recovering from myocardial infarction. *Psychosomatic Medicine, 44,* 519–527.

Bond, G. G., Aiken, L. S., & Somerville, S. C. (1992). The health belief model and adolescents with insulin-dependent diabetes mellitus. *Health Psychology, 11,* 190–198.

Booth-Kewley, S., & Vickers, R. (1994). Associations between major domains of personality and health behavior. *Journal of Personality, 62,* 281–298.

Botelho, R. J., & Dudrak, R. 2nd (1992). Home assessment of adherence to long-term medication in the elderly. *Journal of Family Practice, 35,* 61–65.

Boyd, J. R., Covington, T. R., Stanaszek, W. F., & Coussons, R. T. (1974). Drug defaulting. I. Determinants of compliance. *American Journal of Hospital Pharmacy, 31,* 362–367.

Boyer, C. B., Friend, R., Chlouverakis, G., Kaloyanides, G. (1990). Social support and demographic factors influencing compliance in hemodialysis patients. *Journal of Applied Social Psychology, 20,* 1902–1918.

Brady, B. A., Tucker, C. M., Alfino, P. A., Tarrant, D. G., & Finlayson, G. C. (1997). An investigation of factors associated with fluid adherence among hemodialysis patients: A self-efficacy theory based approach. *Annals of Behavioral Medicine, 19,* 339–343.

Brantley, P. J., Mosley, T. H., Bruce, B. K., McKnight, G. T., & Jones, G. N. (1990). Efficacy of behavioral management and patient education on vascular access cleansing compliance in hemodialysis patients. *Health Psychology, 9,* 103–113.

Brehm, J. W. (1966). *A theory of psychological reactance.* New York: Academic Press.

Brehm, S. S., & Brehm, J. W. (1981). *Psychological reactance.* New York: Wiley.

Brody, D. S. (1980). Physician recognition of behavioral, psychological, and social aspects of medical care. *Archives of Internal Medicine, 140,* 1286–1289.

Brown, J., & Fitzpatrick, R. (1988). Factors influencing compliance with dietary restrictions in dialysis patients. *Journal of Psychosomatic Research, 32,* 191–196.

Burke, L. E., Dunbar-Jacob, J. M., & Hill, M. N. (1997). Compliance with cardiovascular disease prevention strategies: A review of the research. *Annals of Behavioral Medicine, 19,* 239–263.

Burns, J. M., Sneddon, I., Lovell, M., McLean, A., & Martin, B. J. (1992). Elderly patients and their medication: A post-discharge follow-up study. *Age and Ageing, 21,* 178–181.

Bushman, B. J., & Stack, A. D. (1996). Forbidden fruit versus tainted fruit: Effects of warning labels on attraction to television violence. *Journal of Experimental Psychology: Applied, 2,* 207–226.

Carney, R. M., Freedland, K. E., Eisen, S. A., Rich, M. W., Skala, J. A., & Jaffe, A. S. (1998). Adherence to a prophylactic medication regimen in patients with symptomatic versus asymptomatic ischemic heart disease. *Behavioral Medicine, 24,* 35–39.

Carney, R. M., Schechter, K., & Davis, T. (1983). Improving adherence to blood glucose testing in insulin-dependent diabetic children. *Behavior Therapy, 14,* 247–254.

Carton, J. S., & Schweitzer, J. B. (1996). Use of a token economy to increase compliance during hemodialysis. *Journal of Applied Behavioral Analysis, 29,* III–II3.

Caterinicchio, R. P. (1979). Testing plausible path models of interpersonal trust in patient-physician treatment relationships. *Social Science & Medicine, 13A,* 81–99.

Catz, S. L., Kelly, J. A., Bogart, L. M., Benotsch, E. G., & McAuliffe, T. L. (2000). Patterns, correlates, and barriers to medication adherence among persons prescribed new treatments for HIV disease. *Health Psychology, 19,* 124–133.

Centers for Disease Control and Prevention (1994). Medical care expenditures attributable to cigarette smoking. *Morbidity and Mortality Weekly Report, 43,* 469.

Champion, V. L. (1990). Breast self-examination in women 35 and older: A prospective study. *Journal of Behavioral Medicine, 13,* 523–538.

Chen, C. Y., Neufeld, P. S., Feely, C. A., & Skinner, C. S. (1999). Factors influencing compliance with home exercise programs among patients with upper-extremity impairment. *The American Journal of Occupational Therapy, 53,* 171–180.

Chisholm, M. A., Vollenweider, L. J., Mulloy, L. L., Jagadeesan, M., Wynn, J. J., Rogers, H. E., et al. (2000). Renal transplant patient compliance with free immunosuppressive medications. *Transplantation, 70,* 1240–1244.

Choo, P. W., Rand, C. S., Inui, T. S., Lee, M. L., Cain, E., Cordeiro-Breault, M., et al. (1999). Validation of patient reports, automated pharmacy records, and pill counts with electronic monitoring of adherence to antihypertensive therapy. *Medical Care, 37,* 846–857.

Christensen, A. J. (2000). Patient X treatment context interaction in chronic disease: A conceptual framework for the study of patient adherence. *Psychosomatic Medicine, 62,* 435–443.

Christensen, A. J., Edwards, D. L., Moran, P. J., Burke, R., Lounsbury, P., & Gordon, E. (1999a). Cognitive distortion and functional impairment in patients undergoing cardiac rehabilitation. *Cognitive Therapy and Research, 23,* 159–168.

Christensen, A. J., & Ehlers, S. L. (2002). Psychological factors in end-stage renal disease: An emerging context for behavioral medicine research. *Journal of Consulting and Clinical Psychology, 70,* 712–724.

Christensen, A. J., & Johnson, J. (2002). Patient adherence with medical treatment regimens: An interactive approach. *Current Directions in Psychological Science, 11,* 94–97.

Christensen, A. J., & Moran, P. J. (1998). The role of psychosomatic research in the management of end-stage renal disease: A framework for matching patient to treatment. *Journal of Psychosomatic Research, 44,* 523–528.

Christensen, A. J., Moran, P. J., & Ehlers, S. E. (1999). Prediction of future dialysis regimen adherence: A longitudinal test of the patient by treatment interactive model. Paper presented at the annual meeting of the Society of Behavioral Medicine, San Diego.

Christensen, A. J., Moran, P. J., Lawton, W. J., Stallman, D., & Voigts, A. (1997a). Monitoring attentional style and medical regimen adherence. *Health Psychology, 16,* 256–262.

Christensen, A. J., Moran, P. J., & Wiebe, J. S. (1999). Assessment of irrational health beliefs: Relation to health practices and medical regimen adherence. *Health Psychology, 18,* 169–176.

Christensen, A. J., Moran, P. J., Wiebe, J. S., Ehlers, S., & Lawton, W. J. (2002a). Effect of a behavioral self-regulation intervention on patient adherence in hemodialysis. *Health Psychology, 21,* 393–397.

Christensen, A. J., & Smith, T. W. (1995). Personality and patient adherence: Correlates of the Five-Factor Model in renal dialysis. *Journal of Behavioral Medicine, 18,* 305–313.

Christensen, A. J., Smith, T. W., Turner, C. W., & Cundick, K. E. (1994). Patient adherence and adjustment in renal dialysis: A person by treatment interactional approach. *Journal of Behavioral Medicine, 17,* 549–566.

Christensen, A. J., Smith, T. W., Turner. C. W., Holman, J. M., & Gregory, M. C. (1990). Type of hemodialysis and preference for behavioral involvement: Interactive effects on adherence in end-stage renal disease. *Health Psychology, 9,* 225–236.

Christensen, A. J., Smith, T. W., Turner, C. W., Holman, J. M., Gregory, M. C., & Rich, M. A. (1992). Family support, physical impairment, and adherence in hemodialysis: An investigation of main and buffering effects. *Journal of Behavioral Medicine,15,* 313–325.

Christensen, A. J., Turner, C. W., Slaughter, J. R., & Holman, J. M. (1989). Perceived family support as a moderator: Psychological well-being in end-stage renal disease. *Journal of Behavioral Medicine, 12,* 249–265.

Christensen, A. J., Wiebe, J. S., Benotsch, E. G., & Lawton, W. J. (1996). Perceived health competence, health locus of control, and patient adherence in renal dialysis. *Cognitive Therapy and Research, 20,* 411–421.

Christensen, A. J., Wiebe, J. S., & Lawton, W. J. (1997b). Cynical hostility, expectancies about health care providers, and patient adherence in hemodialysis. *Psychosomatic Medicine, 59,* 307–312.

Christensen, A. J., & Wiebe, J. S., Smith, T. W., & Turner, C. W. (1994b). Predictors of survival among hemodialysis patients: Effect of perceived family support. *Health Psychology, 13,* 521–526.

Ciechanowski, P. S., Katon, W. J., & Russo, J. E. (2000). Depression and diabetes: Impact of depressive symptoms on adherence, function, and costs. *Archives of Internal Medicine, 27,* 3278–3285.

Cinti, S. K. (2000). Adherence to antiretrovirals in HIV disease. *The AIDS Reader, 10,* 709–717.

Clark, L. T. (1991). Improving compliance and increasing control of hypertension: Needs of special hypertensive populations. *American Heart Journal, 121,* 664–669.

Cleemput, I., Kesteloot, K., & De Geest, S. (2002). A review of the literature on the economics of noncompliance. Room for methodological improvement. *Health Policy, 59,* 65–94.

Cochran, S. D., & Gitlin, M. J. (1988). Attitudinal correlates of lithium compliance in bipolar affective disorders. *The Journal of Nervous and Mental Disease, 176,* 457–464.

Cockburn, J., Reid, A. L., Bowman, J. A., Sanson-Fisher, R. W. (1987). Effects of intervention on antibiotic compliance in patients in general practice. *Medical Journal of Australia, 147,* 324–328.

Cohen, S., & Wills, T. A. (1985). Stress, social support, and the buffering hypothesis. *Psychological Bulletin, 98,* 310–357.

Col, N., Fanale, J. E., & Kronholm, P. (1990). The role of medication noncompliance and adverse drug reactions in hospitalizations of the elderly. *Archives of Internal Medicine, 150,* 841–845.

Cook, W. W., & Medley, D. M. (1954). Proposed hostility and pharisaic-virtue scales for the MMPI. *Journal of Applied Psychology, 38,* 414–418.

Costa, P. T., & McCrae, R. R. (1992). *NEO PI-R professional manual.* Odessa, Florida: Psychological Assessment Resources, Inc.

Costa, P. T., McCrae, R. R., & Dembroski, T. M. (1989). Agreeableness versus antagonism: Explication of a potential risk factor for CHD. In A. W. Siegman & T. M. Dembroski (Eds.), *In search of coronary-prone behavior* (pp. 41–63). Hillsdale, N.J.: Lawrence Erlbaum Associates.

Cox, D. J., & Gonder-Frederick, L. (1992). Major developments in behavioral diabetes research. *Journal of Consulting and Clinical Psychology, 60,* 628–638.

Cox, D. J., Taylor, A. G., Nowacek, G., Holley-Wilcox, P., Pohl, S. L., Guthrow, E. (1984). The relationship between psychological stress and insulin-dependent diabetic blood glucose control: Preliminary investigations. *Health Psychology, 3,* 63–75.

Cramer, J. A., Mattson, R. H., Prevey, M. L., Scheyer, R. D., & Ouellette, V. L. (1989). How often is medication taken as prescribed? A novel assessment technique. *The Journal of the American Medical Association, 261,* 3273–3277.

Creer, T. L., Backial, M., Burns, K. L., Leung, P., Marion, R. J., Miklich, D. R., Morrill, C., Taplin, P. S., Ullman, S. (1988). Living with asthma. I. Genesis and development of a self-management program for childhood asthma. *The Journal of Asthma, 25,* 335–362.

Cropanzano, R., & Wright, T. A. (2001). When a "happy" worker is really a "productive" worker: A review and further refinement of the happy-productive worker thesis. *Consulting Psychology Journal: Practice & Research, 53,* 182–199.

Cuerdon, T. (2002). Adherence and Behavior Change Program. National Institute of Mental Health. Personal communication.

Cummings, K. M., Becker, M. H., Kirscht, J. P., & Levin, N. W. (1981). Intervention strategies to improve compliance with medical regimens by ambulatory hemodialysis patients. *Journal of Behavioral Medicine, 4,* 111–127.

Cummings, K. M., Jette, A. M., & Brock, B. M. (1984). Psychosocial determinants of immunization behavior in a swine influenza campaign. *Medical Care, 4,* 639–649.

Dance, K. A., & Neufeld, R. W. J. (1988). Aptitude-treatment interaction research in the clinical setting: A review of attempts to dispel the "patient uniformity myth." *Psychology Bulletin, 104,* 192–213.

Davidson, R. J., Pizzagalli, D., Nitschke, J. B., & Putnam, K. (2002). Depression: Perspectives from affective neuroscience. *Annual Review of Psychology, 53,* 545–574.

Davis, M. C., Tucker, C. M., & Fennell, R. S. (1996). Family behavior, adaptation, and treatment adherence of pediatric nephrology patients. *Pediatric Nephrology, 10,* 160–166.

Davison, A. M. (1996). Options in renal replacement therapy. In C. Jacobs, C. Kjellstrand, K. Koch, & J. Winchester (Eds.), *Replacement of renal function by dialysis,* 4th edition (pp. 1304–1315). Boston: Kluwer Academic.

De Geest, S., Borgermans, L., Gemoets, H., Abraham, I., Vlaminck, H., Evers, G., & Vanrenterghem, Y. (1995). Incidence, determinants, and consequences of subclinical noncompliance with immunosuppressive therapy in renal transplant recipients. *Transplantation, 59,* 340–347.

De Groot, M., Jacobson, A. M., Samson, J. A., & Welch, G. (1999). Glycemic control and major depression in patients with type 1 and type 2 diabetes mellitus. *Journal of Psychosomatic Research, 46,* 425–435.

Delmonte, M. M. (1988). Personality correlates of meditation practice frequency and dropout in an outpatient population. *Journal of Behavioral Medicine, 11,* 593–597.

De-Nour, A. K., & Czackes, J. W. (1976). The influence of patient's personality on adjustment to chronic dialysis. *The Journal of Nervous and Mental Disease, 162,* 323–333.

Devine, E. C., & Pearcy, J. (1996). Meta-analysis of the effects of psychoeducational care in adults with chronic obstructive pulmonary disease. *Patient Education Counseling, 29,* 167–178.

De Weerdt, I., Visser, A. P., Kok, G. J., de Weerdt, O., van der Veen, E. A. (1990). Determinants of active self-care behaviour of insulin treated patients with diabetes: Implications for diabetes education. *Social Sciences and Medicine, 30,* 605–615.

De Weerdt, I., Visser, A. P., Kok, G. J., de Weerdt, O., van der Veen, E. A. (1991).

Randomized controlled multicentre evaluation of an education programme for insulin-treated diabetic patients: Effects on metabolic control, quality of life, and costs of therapy. *Diabetic Medicine, 8,* 338–345.

Diabetes Control and Complications Trial (DCCT) Research Group. (1993). The effect of intensive treatment of diabetes on the development and progression of long-term complications in insulin-dependent diabetes mellitus. *New England Journal of Medicine, 329,* 977–986.

Diaz-Buxo, J. A., Plahey, K., & Walker, S. (1999). Memory card: A tool to assess patient compliance in peritoneal dialysis. *Artificial Organs, 23,* 956–958.

Dickinson, J. C., Warshaw, G. A., Gehlbach, S. H., Bobula, J. A., Muhlbaier, L. H., & Parkerson, G. R., Jr. (1981). Improving hypertension control: Impact of computer feedback and physician education. *Medical Care, 19,* 843–854.

Digman, J. M. (1990). Personality structure: Emergence of the five-factor model. *Annual Review of Psychology, 41,* 417–440.

DiMatteo, M. R. (1998). The role of the physician in the emerging health care environment. *Western Journal of Medicine, 168,* 328–333.

DiMatteo, M. R., & DiNicola, D. D. (1982). *Achieving patient compliance.* New York: Pergamon.

DiMatteo, M. R., Sherbourne, C. D., Hays, R. D., Ordway, L., Kravitz, R. L., McGlynn, E. A., et al. (1993). Physicians' characteristics influence patients' adherence to medical treatment: Results from the medical outcomes study. *Health Psychology, 12,* 93–102.

Dimond, M. (1979). Social support and adaptation to chronic illness: The case of maintenance hemodialysis. *Research in Nursing & Health, 2,* 101–108.

Dodrill, C. B., Batzel, L. W., Wilensky, A. J., & Yerby, M. S. (1987). The role of psychosocial and financial factors in medication noncompliance in epilepsy. *International Journal of Psychiatry in Medicine, 17,* 143–154.

Donnell, A. J., Thomas, A., & Buboltz, W. C., Jr. (2001). Psychological reactance: Factor structure and internal consistency of the questionnaire for the measurement of psychological reactance. *The Journal of Social Psychology, 141,* 679–687.

Dubbert, P. M. (1992). Exercise in behavioral medicine. *Journal of Consulting and Clinical Psychology, 60,* 613–618.

Dunbar-Jacob, J., Dwyer, K., & Dunning, E. J. (1991). Compliance with antihypertensive regimen: A review of the research in the 1980s. *Annals of Behavioral Medicine, 13,* 31–39.

Dunbar-Jacob, J., & Schlenk, E. (2001). Patient adherence to treatment regimen. In A. Baum, T. A. Revenson, & J. E. Singer (Eds.), *Handbook of health psychology* (pp. 571–580). Mahwah, N.J.: Lawrence Erlbaum Associates.

Dunbar-Jacob, J., Schlenk, E., Caruthers, D. (2002). Adherence in the management of chronic disorders. In A. Christensen & M. Antoni (Eds.), *Chronic physical disorders: Behavioral medicine's perspective.* Oxford: Blackwell Publishers.

Easton, D. F., Ford D., & Bishop, D. T. (1995). Breast and ovarian cancer incidence in BRCA1-mutation carriers. Breast Cancer Linkage Consortium. *American Journal of Human Genetics, 56,* 265–271.

Edinger, J. D., Carwile, S., Miller, P., Hope, V., & Mayti, C. (1994). Psychological status, syndromatic measures, and compliance with nasal CPAP therapy for sleep apnea. *Perceptual and Motor Skills, 78,* 1116–1118.

Edmonds, D., Foerster, E., Groth, H., Greminger, P., Siegenthaler, W., Vetter, W. (1985). Does self-measurement of blood pressure improve patient compliance in hypertension? *Journal of Hypertension. Supplement, 3,* S31–S34.F.

Edworthy, S. M., Devins, G. M. (1999). Improving medication adherence through patient education distinguishing between appropriate and inappropriate utilization. Patient education study group. *Journal of Rheumatology, 26,* 1793–1801.

Eisenthal, S., Emery, R., Lazare, A., & Udin, H. (1979). "Adherence" and the negotiated approach to patienthood. *Archives of General Psychiatry, 36,* 393–398.

Eitel, P., Friend, R., Griffin, K. W., & Wadhwa, N. K. (1998). Cognitive control and consistency in compliance. *Psychology & Health, 13,* 953–973.

Elixhauser, A., Eisen, S. A., Romeis, J. C., Homan, S. M. (1990). The effects of monitoring and feedback on compliance. *Medical Care, 28,* 882–893.

Elliott, V., Morgan, S., Day, S., Mollerup, L. S., & Wang, W. (2001). Parental health beliefs and compliance with prophylactic penicillin administration in children with sickle cell disease. *Journal of Pediatric Hematology/Oncology, 23,* 112–116.

Engel, G. (1977). The need for a new medical model: A challenge for biomedicine. *Science, 196,* 129–136.

Engel, G. (1980). The clinical application of the biopsychosocial model. *American Journal of Psychiatry, 137,* 535–544.

Engs, R., & Hanson, D. J. (1989). Reactance theory: A test with collegiate drinking. *Psychological Reports, 64,* 1083–1086.

Epstein, L. H., & Clauss, P. A. (1982). A behavioral medicine perspective on adherence to long-term medical regimens. *Journal of Consulting and Clinical Psychology, 50,* 950–971.

Evangelista, L. S., Berg, J., & Dracup, K. (2001). Relationship between psychosocial variables and compliance in patients with heart failure. *Heart Lung, 30,* 294–301.

Everly, G. S., Jr., & Newman, E. C. (1997). The MBHI: Composition and clinical applications. In T. Millon (Ed.), *The million inventories: Clinical and personality assessment* (pp. 389–408). New York and London: Guilford Press.

Ewart, C. K. (1992). Role of physical self-efficacy in recovery from heart attack. In R. Schwarzer (Ed.), *Self-efficacy: Thought control of action* (pp. 287–304). Washington, D.C.: Hemisphere Publishing.

Farmer, K. C. (1999). Methods for measuring and monitoring medication regimen adherence in clinical trials and clinical practice. *Clinical Therapeutics, 21,* 1074–1090.

Feely, M., Cooke, J., Price, D., Singleton, S., Mehta, A., Bradford, L., & Calvert, R. (1987). Low-dose phenobarbitone as an indicator of compliance with drug therapy. *British Journal of Clinical Pharmacology, 24,* 77–83.

Feinstein, A. R. (1990). On white-coat effects and the electronic monitoring of compliance. *Archives of Internal Medicine, 150,* 1377–1378.

Ferster, C. B., Nurnberger, J. I., & Levitt, E. B. (1962). The control of eating. *Journal of Mathematics, 1,* 87–109.

Fincham, J. E., & Wertheimer, A. I. (1985). Using the health belief model to predict initial drug therapy defaulting. *Social Science & Medicine, 20,* 101–105.

Finnegan, D. L., & Suler, J. R. (1985). Psychological factors associated with maintenance of improved health behaviors in postcoronary patients. *Journal of Psychology, 119,* 87–94.

Finney, J. W., Friman, P. C., Rapoff, M. A., Christophersen, E. R. (1985). Improving compliance with antibiotic regimens for otitis media. Randomized clinical trial in a pediatric clinic. *American Journal of Diseases of Children, 139,* 89–95.

Floyd, D. L., Prentice-Dunn, S., & Rogers, R. W. (2000). A meta-analysis on protection motivation theory. *Journal of Applied Social Psychology, 30,* 407–429.

Fogarty, L., Roter, D., Larson, S., Burke, J., Gillespie, J., & Levy, R. (2002). Patient adherence to HIV medication regimens: A review of published and abstract reports. *Patient Education Counseling, 46,* 93–108.

Fogarty, J. S., & Youngs, G. A., Jr. (2000). Psychological reactance as a factor in patient noncompliance with medication taking: A field experiment. *Journal of Applied Social Psychology, 30,* 2365–2391.

Frankenhauser, M. (1975). Sympathetic adrenomedullary activity and the psychosocial environment. In P. Venables & M. Christie (Eds.), *Research in psychophysiology* (pp. 71–94). New York: Wiley.

Frick, P. A., Gal, P., Lane, T. W., & Sewell, P. C. (1998). Antiretroviral medication compliance in patients with AIDS. *AIDS Patient Care and STDS, 12,* 463–470.

Friedman, M., & Rosenman, R. H. (1974). *Type A behavior and your heart.* New York: Knopf.

Friend, R., Hatchett, L., Schneider, M. S., & Wadhwa, N. K. (1997). A comparison of attributions, health beliefs, and negative emotions as predictors of fluid adherence in renal dialysis patients: A prospective analysis. *Annals of Behavioral Medicine, 19,* 344–347.

Funch, D. P., & Gale, E. N. (1986). Predicting treatment completion in a behavioral therapy program for chronic temporomandibular pain. *Journal of Psychosomatic Research, 30,* 57–62.

Galatzer, A., Amir, S., Gil, R., Karp, M., & Laron, Z. (1982). Crisis intervention program in newly diagnosed diabetic children. *Diabetes Care, 5,* 414–419.

Gallefoss, F., & Bakke, P. S. (1999). How does patient education and self-management among asthmatics and patients with chronic obstructive pulmonary disease affect medication? *American Journal of Respiratory and Critical Care Medicine, 160,* 2000–2005.

Garrity, T. F., & Garrity, A. R. (1985). The nature and efficacy of intervention studies in the National High Blood Pressure Education Research Program. *Journal of Hypertension. Supplement, 3,* S91–S95.

Girvin, B., McDermott, B. J., & Johnston, G. D. (1999). A comparison of enalapril 20 mg once daily versus 10 mg twice daily in terms of blood pressure lowering and patient compliance. *Journal of Hypertension, 17,* 1627–1631.

Glasgow, R. E., McCaul, K. D., Schafer, L. C. (1986). Barriers to regimen adherence among persons with insulin-dependent diabetes. *Journal of Behavioral Medicine, 6,* 65–77.

Glasgow, R. E., McCaul, K. D., & Schafer, L. C. (1987). Self-care behaviors and glycemic control in type I diabetes. *Journal of Chronic Diseases, 40,* 399–412.

Glass, D. C., & Singer, J. E. (1972). *Urban stress.* New York: Academic Press.

Godin, G. (1993). The theories of reasoned action and planned behavior: Overview of findings, emerging research problems, and usefulness for exercise promotion. *Journal of Applied Sport Psychology, 5,* 141–157.

Godin, G., Valois, P., & LePage, L. (1993). The pattern of influence of perceived behavioral control upon exercising behavior: An application of Ajzen's theory of planned behavior. *Journal of Behavioral Medicine, 16,* 81–102.

Goldberg, A. I., Cohen, G., & Rubin, A. H. (1998). Physician assessments of patient compliance with medical treatment. *Social Science & Medicine, 47,* 1873–1876.

Goldstein, M. S., Jaffe, D. T., Sutherland, C., & Wilson, J. (1987). Holistic physicians: Implications for the study of the medical profession. *Journal of Health and Social Behavior, 28,* 103–119.

Grady, K. E., Goodenow, C., & Borkin, J. R. (1988). The effect of reward on compliance with breast self-examination. *Journal of Behavioral Medicine, 11,* 43–57.

Graveley, E. A., & Oseasohn, C. S. (1991). Multiple drug regimens: Medication compliance among veterans 65 years and older. *Research in Nursing & Health, 14,* 51–58.

Grey, M., Boland, E. A., Davidson, M., Yu, C., Sullivan-Bolyai, S., Tamborlane, W. V. (1998). Short-term effects of coping skills training as adjunct to intensive therapy in adolescents. *Diabetes Care, 21,* 902–908.

Griffith, L. S., Field, B. J., & Lustman, P. J. (1990). Life stress and social support in diabetes: Association with glycemic control. *International Journal of Psychiatry in Medicine, 20,* 365–372.

Gross, D. A., Zyzanski, S. J., Borawski, E. A., Cebul, R. D., & Stange, K. C. (1998). Patient satisfaction with time spent with their physician. *The Journal of Family Practice, 47,* 133–137.

Hall, J. A., Roter, D. L., & Katz, N. R. (1988). Meta-analysis of correlates of provider behavior in medical encounters. *Medical Care, 26,* 657–675.

Hamilton, R. A., & Briceland, L. L. (1992). Use of prescription-refill records to assess patient compliance. *American Journal of Hospital Pharmacy, 49,* 1691–1696.

Hanson, C. L., Henggeler, S. W., & Burgehn, G. A. (1987). Social competence and parental support as mediators of the link between stress and metabolic control in adolescents with insulin-dependent diabetes mellitus. *Journal of Consulting and Clinical Psychology, 55,* 529–533.

Harlan, W. R., 3rd, Sandler, S. A., Lee, K. L., Lam, L. C., & Mark, D. B. (1995). Importance of baseline functional and socioeconomic factors for participation in cardiac rehabilitation. *The American Journal of Cardiology, 76,* 36–39.

Harper, R. G., Chacko, R. C., Kotik-Harper, D., Young, J., & Gotto, J. (1998). Self-report evaluation of health behavior, stress vulnerability, and medical outcome of heart transplant recipients. *Psychosomatic Medicine, 60,* 563–569.

Hart, R. (1979). Utilization of token economy within a chronic dialysis unit. *Journal of Consulting and Clinical Psychology, 47,* 646–648.

Hatcher, M. E., Green, L. W., Levine, D. M., & Flagle, C. E. (1986). Validation of a decision model for triaging hypertensive patients to alternate health education interventions. *Social Science and Medicine, 22,* 813–819.

Haug, M. R. (1997). Physician power and patients' health behavior. In D. S. Gochman (Ed.), *Handbook of health behavior research II: Provider determinants* (pp. 49–62). New York: Plenum Press.

Hawe, P., & Higgins, G. (1990). Can medication education improve the drug compliance of the elderly? *Patient Education Counseling, 16,* 151–160.

Haynes, R. B. (1979). Determinants of compliance: The disease and the mechanics of treatment. In R. B. Haynes, D. W. Taylor, & D. L. Sackett (Eds.), *Compliance in healthcare* (pp. 49–62). Baltimore: Johns Hopkins University Press.

Haynes, R. B., Montague, P., Oliver, T., McKibbon, K. A., Brouwers, M. C., & Kanani, R. (2002). Interventions for helping patients to follow prescriptions for medications (Cochrane review). In *The Cochrane Library,* Issue 1, 2002. Oxford: Update Software.

Haynes, R. B., Sackett, D. L., Gibson, E. S., Taylor, D. W., Hackett, B. C.,

Roberts, R. S., Johnson, A. L. (1976). Improvement of mediation compliance in uncontrolled hypertension. *Lancet, 1,* 1265–1268.

Hegel, M. T., Ayllon, T., Thiel, G., & Oulton, B. (1992). Improving adherence to fluid-restrictions in male hemodialysis patients: A comparison of cognitive and behavioral approaches. *Health Psychology, 11,* 324–330.

Herman, C. J., Speroff, T., Cebul, R. D. (1994). Improving compliance with immunization in the older adult: Results of a randomized cohort study. *Journal of the American Geriatrics Society, 42,* 1154–1159.

Hershberger, P. J., Robertson, K. B., & Markert, R. J. (1999). Personality and appointment-keeping adherence in cardiac rehabilitation. *Journal of Cardiopulmonary Rehabilitation, 19,* 106–111.

Higgins, E. T. (1990). Personality, social psychology, and person-situation relations: Standards and knowledge activation as a common language. In L. A. Pervin (Ed.), *Handbook of personality: Theory and research* (pp. 301–338). New York: Guilford Press.

Hitchcock, P. B., Brantley, P. J., Jones, G. N., & McKnight, G. T. (1992). Stress and social support as predictors of dietary compliance in hemodialysis patients. *Behavioral Medicine, 18,* 13–20.

Hochbaum, G. M. (1958). *Public participation in medical screening programs: A sociopsychological study.* PHS Publication No. 572. Washington, D.C.: U.S. Government Printing Office.

Hong, S. (1992). Hong's Psychological Reactance Scale: A further factor analytic validation. *Psychological Reports, 70,* 512–514.

Horne, R., & Weinman, J. (1999). Patients' beliefs about prescribed medicines and their role in adherence to treatment in chronic physical illness. *Journal of Psychosomatic Research, 47,* 555–567.

Jacobson, N. S., Roberts, L. J., Berns, S. B., & McGlinchey, J. B. (1999). Methods for defining and determining the clinical significance of treatment effects: Description, application, and alternatives. *Journal of Consulting and Clinical Psychology, 67,* 300–307.

Janis, I. L. (1984). Improving adherence to medical recommendations: Prescriptive hypotheses derived from recent research in social psychology. In A. Baum, S. Taylor, J. Singer (Eds.), *Handbook of psychology and health,* vol. 4: *Social psychological aspects of health* (pp. 113–146). Hillside, N.J.: Lawrence Erlbaum Associates.

Jay, M. S., DuRant, R. H., Shoffitt, T., Linder, C. W., & Litt, I. F. (1984). Effect of peer counselors on adolescent compliance in use of oral contraceptives. *Pediatrics, 73,* 126–131.

Jenkins, C. D., Zyzanski, S. J., & Rosenman, R. H. (1979). *Jenkins Activity Survey.* Cleveland, Ohio: Psychological Corporation.

Jensen, K., Banwart, L., Venhaus, R., Popkess-Vawter, S., & Perkins, S. B. (1993). Advanced rehabilitation nursing care of coronary angioplasty patients using self-efficacy theory. *Journal of Advanced Nursing, 18,* 926–931.

Johnson, A. L., Taylor, D. W., Sackett, D. L., Dunnett, C. W., Shimizu, A. G. (1978). Self-recording of blood pressure in the management of hypertension. *Canadian Medical Association Journal, 119,* 1034–1039.

Jones, P. K., Jones, S. L., Katz, J. (1987). Improving follow-up among hypertensive patients using a health belief model intervention. *Archives of Internal Medicine, 147,* 1557–1560.

Jornsay, D. L., Duckles, A. E., & Hankinson, J. P. (1988). Psychological considerations for patient selection and adjustment to insulin pump therapy. *The Diabetes Educator, 14,* 291–296.

Kanfer, F. H., & Gaelick, L. (1986). Self-management methods. In F. Kanfer & A. Goldstein (Eds.), *Helping people change:* 3rd edition. New York: Pergamon Press.

Kaplan, R. M., Atkins, C. J., & Reinsch, S. (1984). Specific efficacy expectations mediate exercise compliance in patients with COPD. *Health Psychology, 3,* 223–242.

Kaplan, R. M., Chadwick, M. W., Schimmel, L. E. (1985). Social learning intervention to promote metabolic control in type I diabetes mellitus: Pilot experiment results. *Diabetes Care, 8,* 152–155.

Kaplan, R. M., & Hartwell, S. L. (1987). Differential effects of social support and social network on physiological and social outcomes in men and women with type II diabetes mellitus. *Health Psychology, 6,* 387–398.

Kaplan, R. M., & Simon, H. J. (1990). Compliance in medical care: Reconsideration of self-predictions. *Annals of Behavioral Medicine, 12,* 66–71.

Karvetti, R. L. (1981). Effects of nutrition education. *Journal of the American Dietetic Association, 79,* 660–667.

Kavanagh, D. J., Gooley, S., & Wilson, P. H. (1993). Prediction of adherence and control in diabetes. *Journal of Behavioral Medicine, 16,* 509–522.

Kayser, J., Ettinger, B., & Pressman, A. (2001). Postmenopausal support: Discontinuation of raloxifene versus estrogen. *Menopause, 8,* 328–332.

Kelly, G. R., Scott, J. E., Mamon, J. (1990). Medication compliance and health education among outpatients with chronic mental disorders. *Medical Care, 28,* 1181–1197.

Kelly, J. A., & Kalichman, S. C. (2002). *Journal of Consulting and Clinical Psychology, 70,* 626–639.

Kendall, P. C. (1999). Clinical significance. *Journal of Consulting and Clinical Psychology, 67,* 283–284.

Kendall, P. C., Marrs-Garcia, A., Nath, S. R., & Sheldrick, R. C. (1999). Normative comparisons for the evaluation of clinical significance. *Journal of Consulting and Clinical Psychology, 67,* 285–299.

Kerns, R. K., & Weiss, L. H. (1994). Family influences on the course of chronic illness: A cognitive-behavioral transactional model. *Annals of Behavioral Medicine, 16,* 116–121.

Keegan, J. F., Dewey, D., & Lucas, C. P. (1987). MMPI correlates of medical compliance in a weight control program. *International Journal of Eating Disorders, 6,* 439–442.

Kiley, D. J., Lam, C. S., & Pollak, R. (1993). A study of treatment compliance following kidney transplantation. *Transplantation, 55,* 51–56.

Kimmel, P. L., Peterson, R. A., Weihs, K. L., Simmens, S. J., Boyle, D. H., Verme, D., et al. (1995). Behavioral compliance with dialysis prescription in hemodialysis patients. *Journal of the American Society of Nephrology, 5,* 1826–1834.

Kimmel, P. L., Varela, M. P., Peterson, R. A., Weihs, K. L., Simmens, S. J., Alleyne, S., et al. (2000). Interdialytic weight gain and survival in hemodialysis patients: Effects of duration of ESRD and diabetes mellitus. *Kidney International, 57,* 1141–1151.

King, A. C., Taylor, C. B., Haskell, W. L., Debusk, R. F. (1988). Strategies for increasing early adherence to and long-term maintenance of home-based exercise training in healthy middle-aged men and women. *The American Journal of Cardiology, 61,* 628–632.

Kinsman, R. A., Dirks, J. F., & Dahlem, N. W. (1980). Noncompliance to prescribed-as-needed (PRN) medication use in asthma: Usage patterns and patient characteristics. *Journal of Psychosomatic Research, 24,* 97–107.

Kirscht, J. P., Kirscht, J. L., & Rosenstock, I. M. (1981). A test of interventions to increase adherence to hypertensive medical regimens. *Health Education Quarterly, 8,* 261–272.

Kotses, H., Bernstein, I. L., Bernstein, D. I., Reynolds, R. V., Korbee, L., Wigal, J. K., Ganson, E., Stout, C., Creer, T. L. (1995). A self-management program for adult asthma. Part I: Development and evaluation. *The Journal of Allergy and Clinical Immunology, 95,* 529–540.

Krantz, D. S., Baum, A., & Wideman, M. V. (1980). Assessment of preferences for self-treatment and information in health care. *Journal of Personality and Social Psychology, 39,* 977–990.

Kulik, J. A., & Carlino, P. (1987). The effect of verbal commitment and treatment choice on medication compliance in a pediatric setting. *Journal of Behavioral Medicine, 10,* 367–376.

Kulik, J. A., & Mahler, H. I. (1993). Emotional support as a moderator of adjustment and compliance after coronary artery bypass surgery: A longitudinal study. *Journal of Behavioral Medicine, 16,* 45–63.

Lane, J. D., McCaskill, C. C., Williams, P. G., Parekh, P. I., Feinglos, M. N., & Surwit, R. S. (2000). Personality correlates of glycemic control on type 2 diabetes. *Diabetes Care, 23,* 1321–1325.

Leclercq, R. (2001). Safeguarding future antimicrobial options: Strategies to minimize resistance. *Clinical Microbiology and Infection, 7,* 18–23.

Lee, J. Y., Greene, P. G., Douglas, M., Grim, C., Kirk, K. A., Kusek, J. W., et al. (1996). Appointment attendance, pill counts, and achievement of goal blood pressure in the African American study of kidney disease and hypertension pilot study. *Controlled Clinical Trials, 17,* 34S–39S.

Leermakers, E. A., Dunn, A. L., & Blair, S. N. (2000). Exercise management of obesity. *Medical Clinics of North America, 84,* 419–440.

Lerman, C., Ross, E., Boyce, A., Gorchov, P. M., McLaughlin, R., Rimer, B., & Engstrom, P. (1992). The impact of mailing psychoeducational materials to women with abnormal mammograms. *American Journal of Public Health, 82,* 729–730.

Levine, D. M. (1982). Health education for behavioral change: Clinical trial to public health program. *Johns Hopkins Medical Journal, 151,* 215–219.

Levine, D. M., Green, L. W., Deeds, S. G., Chwalow, J., Russell, R. P., Finlay, J. (1979). Health education for hypertensive patients. *Journal of the American Medical Association, 241,* 1700–1703.

Levy, R. (1983). Social support and compliance: A selective review and critique of treatment integrity and outcome measurement. *Social Science & Medicine, 17,* 1329–1338.

Li, B. D., Brown, W. A., Ampil, F. L., Burton, G. V., Yu, H., & McDonald, J. C. (2000). Patient compliance is critical for equivalent clinical outcomes for breast cancer treated by breast-conservation therapy. *Annals of Surgery, 231,* 883–889.

Lipsey, M. W., & Wilson, D. B. (1993). The efficacy of psychological, educational, and behavioral treatment: Confirmation from meta-analysis. *American Psychologist, 48,* 1181–1209.

Liptak, G. S. (1996). Enhancing patient compliance in pediatrics. *Pediatrics in Review, 17,* 128–134.

Littlefield, C. H., Craven, J. L., Rodin, G. M., Daneman, D., Murray, M. A., & Rydall, A. C. (1992). Relationship of self-efficacy and binging to adherence to diabetes regimen among adolescents. *Diabetes Care, 15,* 90–94.

Lloyd, C. E., Wing, R. R., Orchard, T. J., & Becker, D. J. (1993). Psychosocial correlates of glycemic control: The Pittsburgh epidemiology of diabetes complications (EDC) study. *Diabetes Research and Clinical Practice, 21,* 187–195.

Lustman, P. J., Anderson, R. J., Freedland, K. E., de Groot, M., Carney, R. M., & Clouse, R. E. (2000). Depression and poor glycemic control: A meta-analytic review of the literature. *Diabetes Care, 23,* 934–942.

Lynch, D. J., Birk, T. J., Weaver, M. T., Gohara, A. F., Leighton, R. F., Repka, F. J., & Walsh, M. E. (1992). Adherence to exercise interventions in the treatment of hypercholesterolemia. *Journal of Behavioral Medicine, 15,* 365–377.

Madden, T. J., Ellen, P. S., & Ajzen, I. (1992). A comparison of the theory of planned behavior and the theory of reasoned action. *Personality and Social Psychology Bulletin, 1,* 3–9.

Maddux, J. E., & DuCharme, K. A. (1997). Behavioral intentions in theories of health behavior. In D. S. Gochman (Ed.), *Handbook of health behavior research I: Personal and social determinants* (pp. 133–151). New York: Plenum Press.

Maiman, L. A., Green, L. W., Gibson, G., MacKenzie, E. J. (1979). Education for self-treatment by adult asthmatics. *Journal of the American Medical Association, 241,* 1919–1922.

Mallion, J. M., Baguet, J. P., Siche, J. P., Tremel, F., & de Gaudemaris, R. (1998). Compliance, electronic monitoring and antihypertensive drugs. *Journal of Hypertension. Supplement, 16,* S75–S79.

Manley, M., & Sweeney, J. (1986). Assessment of compliance in hemodialysis adaptation. *Journal of Psychosomatic Research, 30,* 153–161.

Marcus, A. O., & Fernandez, M. P. (1996). Insulin pump therapy: Acceptable alternative to injection therapy. *Postgraduate Medicine, 99,* 125–132.

Marshall, L. L., & Roiger, R. J. (1996). Substance user MMPI-2 profiles: Predicting failure in completing treatment. *Substance Use & Misuse, 31,* 197–206.

Martelli, M. E., Auerbach, S. M., Alexander, J., & Mercuri, L. G. (1987). Stress management in the health care setting: Matching interventions with patient coping styles. *Journal of Consulting & Clinical Psychology, 55,* 201–207.

Mattar, M. E., Markello, J., & Yaffe, S. J. (1975). Pharmaceutic factors affecting pediatric compliance. *Pediatrics, 55,* 101–108.

Matthews, K. A. (1988). Coronary heart disease and type A behaviors: Update on and alternative to the booth-kewley and friedman (1987) quantitative review. *Psychological Bulletin, 104,* 373–380.

Mawhinney, H., Spector, S. L., Heitjan, D., Kinsman, R. A., Dirks, J. F., & Pines, I. (1993). As-needed medication use in asthma usage patterns and patient characteristics. *The Journal of Asthma, 30,* 61–71.

McAuley, E., Courneya, K. S., Rudolph, D. L., & Lox, C. L. (1994). Enhancing exercise adherence in middle-aged males and females. *Preventive Medicine, 23,* 498–506.

McCaul, K. D., Glasgow, R. E., & O'Neill, H. K. (1992). The problem of creating habits: Establishing health-protective dental behaviors. *Health Psychology, 11,* 101–110.

McCombs, J. S., Nichol, M. B., Newman, C. M., & Sclar, D. A. (1994). The costs of interrupting antihypertensive drug therapy in a Medicaid population. *Medical Care, 32,* 214–226.

McDonald-Miszczak, L., Maki, S. A., & Gould, O. N. (2000). Self-reported medication adherence and health status in late adulthood: The role of beliefs. *Experimental Aging Research, 26,* 189–207.

McNaughton, K. L., & Rodrigue, J. R. (2001). Predicting adherence to recommendations by parents of clinic-referred children. *Journal of Consulting and Clinical Psychology, 69,* 262–270.

Meichenbaum, D. H., & Turk, D. C. (1987). *Facilitating treatment adherence: A practitioner's guidebook.* New York: Plenum Press.

Milgrom, H., Bender, B., Ackerson, L., Bowry, P., Smith, B., & Rand, C. (1996). Noncompliance and treatment failure in children with asthma. *The Journal of Allergy and Clinical Immunology, 98,* 1051–1057.

Miller, P., Wikoff, R., McMahon, M., Garrett, M. J., & Ringel, K. (1988). Influence of a nursing intervention on regimen adherence and societal adjustments postmyocardial infarction. *Nursing Research, 37,* 297–302.

Miller, S. M., & Mangan, C. E. (1983). Interacting effects of information and coping style in adapting to gynecologic stress: Should the doctor tell all? *Journal of Personality & Social Psychology, 45,* 223–236.

Miller, T. Q., Turner, C. W., Tindale, R. S., Posavac, E. J., & Dugoni, B. L. (1991). Reasons for the trend toward null findings in research on Type A Behavior. *Psychological Bulletin, 110,* 469–485.

Millon, T., Green, C. J., & Meagher, R. B. (1982). A new psychodiagnostic tool for clients in rehabilitation settings: The MBHI. *Rehabilitation Psychology, 27,* 23–35.

Mirotznik, J., Ginzler, E., Zagon, G., & Baptiste, A. (1998). Using the health belief model to explain clinic appointment-keeping for the management of a chronic disease condition. *Journal of Community Health, 23,* 195–210.

Monane, M., Bohn, R. L., Gurwitz, J. H., Glynn, R. J., Levin, R., & Avorn, J. (1996). Compliance with antihypertensive therapy among elderly Medicaid enrollees: The roles of age, gender, and race. *American Journal of Public Health, 86,* 1805–1808.

Montgomery, S., Joseph, J., Becker, M., Ostrow, D., Kessler, R., & Kirscht, J. (1989). The health belief model in understanding compliance with preventive recommendations for AIDS: How useful? *AIDS Education and Prevention, 1,* 303–323.

Moore, A., Sellwood, W., & Stirling, J. (2000). Compliance and psychological reactance in schizophrenia. *British Journal of Clinical Psychology, 39,* 287–295.

Moran, P. J., Christensen, A. J., & Lawton, W. J. (1997). Conscientiousness, social support, and adaptation to chronic illness. *Annals of Behavioral Medicine, 19,* 333–338.

Morduchowicz, G., Sulkes, J., Aizic, S., Gabbay, U., Winkler, J., & Boner, G. (1993). Compliance in hemodialysis patients: A multivariate regression analysis. *Nephron, 64,* 365–368.

Morisky, D. E., DeMuth, N. M., Field-Fass, M., Green, L. W., & Levine, D. M. (1985). Evaluation of family health education to build social support for long-term control of high blood pressure. *Health Education Quarterly, 12,* 35–50.

Morisky, D. E., Levine, D. M., Green, L. W., Russell, R. P., Smith, C., Benson, P., & Finlay, J. (1980). The relative impact of health education for low- and high-risk patients with hypertension. *Preventive Medicine, 9,* 550–558.

Myers, L. B., & Myers, F. (1999). The relationship between control beliefs and self-reported adherence in adults with cystic fibrosis. *Psychology Health & Medicine, 4,* 387–391.

Nathan, P. E., & Gorman, J. M. (2002). Efficacy, effectiveness, and the clinical utility of psychotherapy research. In P. Nathan & J. Gorman (Eds.), *A guide to treatments that work* (pp. 643–654). New York: Oxford University Press.

Nathan, P. E., Stuart, S. P., & Dolan, S. L. (2000). Research on psychotherapy efficacy and effectiveness: Between Scylla and Charybdis. *Psychological Bulletin, 126,* 964–981.

National Institute on Drug Abuse (1992). NIDA InfoFacts: Costs to society. Bethesda, Md.: National Institutes of Health.

Nessman, D. G., Carnahan, J. E., & Nugent, C. A. (1980). Increasing compliance. Patient-operated hypertension groups. *Archives of Internal Medicine, 140,* 1427–1430.

Nicassio, P. M., & Greenberg, M. A. (2001). The effectiveness of cognitive-behavioral and psychoeducational interventions in the management of arthritis. In M. H. Weisman and J. Louie (Eds.), *Treatment of the Rheumatic Diseases* (2nd Ed.) (pp. 147–161). Orlando, Fla.: William Saunders.

Nieuwkerk, P. T., Sprangers, M. A., Burger, D. M., Hoetelmans, R. M., Hugen, P. W., Danner, S. A., et al. (2001). Limited patient adherence to highly active antiretroviral therapy for HIV-1 infection in an observational cohort study. *Archives of Internal Medicine, 161,* 1962–1968.

Noland, M. P. (1989). The effects of self-monitoring and reinforcement on exercise adherence. *Research Quarterly for Exercise & Sport, 60,* 216–224.

Norell, S. E. (1981). Accuracy of patient interviews and estimates by clinical staff in determining medication compliance. *Social Science & Medicine, 15,* 57–61.

Norman, P., & Smith, L. (1995). The theory of planned behavior and exercise: An investigation into the role of prior behaviour, behavioural intentions and attitude variability. *European Journal of Social Psychology, 25,* 403–415.

O'Callaghan, F. V., Chant, D. C., Callan, V. J., & Baglioni, A. (1997). Modes of alcohol use by young adults: An examination of various attitude-behavior theories. *Journal of Studies of Alcohol, 58,* 502–507.

Oldenburg, B., Macdonald, G. J., & Perkins, R. J. (1988). Prediction of quality of life in a cohort of end-stage renal disease patients. *Journal of Clinical Epidemiology, 41,* 555–564.

Oldridge, N. B., & Jones, N. L. (1986). Preventive use of exercise rehabilitation after myocardial infarction. *Acta Med Scand. Supplement, 711,* S123–S129.

Orne, C. M., & Binik, Y. M. (1989). Consistency of adherence across regimen demands. *Health Psychology, 8,* 27–43.

Oygard, L., & Rise, J. (1996). Predicting the intention to eat healthier food among young adults. *Health Education Research, 11,* 453–461.

Padgett, D., Mumford, E., Hynes, M., Carter, R. (1988). Meta-analysis of the effects of educational and psychosocial interventions on management of diabetes mellitus. *Journal of Clinical Epidemiology, 41,* 1007–1030.

Paes, A. H., Bakker, A., & Soe-Agnie, C. J. (1997). Impact of dosage frequency on patient compliance. *Diabetes Care, 20,* 1512–1517.

Paes, A. H., Bakker, A., & Soe-Agnie, C. J. (1998). Measurement of patient compliance. *Pharmacy World & Science, 20,* 73–77.

Parsons, T. (1954). The professions and the social structure. In T. Parsons, *Essay in sociological theory* (pp. 34–49). New York: Free Press.

Petry, N. M., Martin, B., Cooney, J. L., & Kranzler, H. R. (2000). Give them prizes and they will come: Contingency management for treatment of alcohol dependence. *Journal of Consulting and Clinical Psychology, 68,* 250–257.

Pichichero, M. E., Casey, J. R., Mayes, T., Francis, A. B., Marsocci, S. M., Murphy, A. M., & Hoeger, W. (2000). Penicillin failure in streptococcal tonsillopharyngitis: Causes and remedies. *The Pediatric Infectious Disease Journal, 19,* 917–923.

Poll, I. B., & Kaplan De-Nour, A. (1980). Locus of control and adjustment to chronic hemodialysis. *Psychological Medicine, 10,* 153–157.

Pullar, T., Birtwell, A. J., Wiles, P. G., Hay, A., & Feely, M. P. (1988). Use of a pharmacologic indicator to compare compliance with tablets prescribed to be taken once, twice, or three times daily. *Clinical Pharmacology and Therapeutics, 44,* 540–545.

Putnam, D. E., Finney, J. W., Barkley, P. L., & Bonner, M. J. (1994). Enhancing commitment improves adherence to a medical regimen. *Journal of Consulting and Clinical Psychology, 62,* 191–194.

Rabkin, S. W., Boyko, E., Wilson, A., Streja, D. A. (1983). A randomized clinical trial comparing behavior modification and individual counseling in the nutritional therapy of non-insulin-dependent diabetes mellitus: Comparison of the effect on blood sugar, body weight, and serum lipids. *Diabetes Care, 6,* 50–56.

Raiz, L. R., Kilty, K. M., Henry, M. L., & Ferguson, R. M. (1999). Medication compliance following renal transplantation. *Transplantation, 68,* 51–55.

Rapoff, M. A., Purviance, M. R., & Lindsley, C. B. (1988). Educational and behavioral strategies for improving medication compliance in juvenile rheumatoid arthritis. *Archives of Physical Medicine and Rehabilitation, 69,* 439–441.

Redd, M., & de Castro, J. M. (1992). Social facilitation of eating: Effects of social instruction on food intake. *Physiology & Behavior, 52,* 749–754.

Reichert, S., Simon, T., & Halm, E. A. (2000). Physicians' attitudes about prescribing and knowledge of the costs of common medications. *Archives of Internal Medicine, 160,* 2799–2803.

Reid, D. (1984). Participatory control and the chronic illness adjustment process. In H. Lefcourt (Ed.), *Research with the locus of control construct: Extensions and limitations* (pp. 361–389). New York: Academic Press.

Reid, L. D., & Christensen, D. B. (1988). A psychosocial perspective in the explanation of patients' drug-taking behavior. *Social Science & Medicine, 27,* 277–285.

Reinecke, J., Schmidt, P., & Ajzen, I. (1996). Application of the theory of planned behavior to adolescents' condom use: A panel study. *Journal of Applied Social Psychology, 26,* 749–772.

Reynolds, L. R. (2000). Reemergence of insulin pump therapy in the 1990s. *Southern Medical Journal, 93,* 1157–1161.

Rhodewalt, F., & Fairfield, M. (1990). An alternative approach to Type A behavior and health: Psychological reactance and medical noncompliance. *Journal of Social Behavior and Personality, 5,* 323–342.

Rhodewalt, F., & Marcroft, M. (1988). Type A behavior and diabetic control: Implications of psychological reactance for health outcomes. *Journal of Applied Social Psychology, 18,* 139–159.

Rhodewalt, F., & Strube, M. (1985). A self-attribution reactance model of recovery from injury in Type A individuals. *Journal of Applied Social Psychology, 15,* 330–344.

Rich, M. W., Gray, D. B., Beckham, V., Wittenberg, C., & Luther, P. (1996). Effect of a multidisciplinary intervention on medication compliance in elderly patients with congestive heart failure. *American Journal of Medicine, 101,* 270–276.

Richardson, M. A., Simons-Morton, B., & Annegers, J. E. (1993). Effect of perceived barriers on compliance with antihypertensive medication. *Health Education Quarterly, 20,* 489–503.

Rigsby, M. O., Rosen, M. I., Beauvais, J. E., Cramer, J. A., Rainey, P. M., O'Malley, S. S., Dieckhaus, K. D., & Rounsaville, B. J. (2000). Cue-dose training with monetary reinforcement: Pilot study of an antiretroviral adherence intervention. *Journal of General Internal Medicine, 15,* 841–847.

Rimer, B., Levy, M. H., Keintz, M. K., Fox, L., Engstrom, P. F., & MacElwee, N. (1987). Enhancing cancer pain control regimens through patient education. *Patient Education Counseling, 10,* 267–277.

Robin, A. L., Foster, S. L. (1989). *Negotiating Parent-Adolescent Conflict: A Behavioral Family Systems Approach.* New York: Guilford Press.

Robison, F. (1993). A training and support group for elderly diabetics: Description and evaluation. *Journal for Specialists in Group Work, 18,* 127–136.

Rogers, R. W. (1975). A protection motivation theory of fear appeals and attitude change. *The Journal of Psychology, 91,* 93–114.

Rogers, R. W. (1983). Cognitive and physiological processes in fear-based attitude change: A revised theory of protection motivation. In J. Cacioppo & R. Petty (Eds.), *Social psychophysiology: A sourcebook* (pp. 153–176). New York: Guilford Press.

Rogers, R. W., & Prentice-Dunn, S. (1997). Protection motivation theory. In D. S. Gochman (Ed.), *Handbook of health behavior research I: Personal and social determinants* (pp. 113–132). New York: Plenum Press.

Ronis, D. (1992). Conditional health threats: Health beliefs, decisions, and behaviors among adults. *Health Psychology, 11*, 127–134.

Rosenbaum, M., & Ben-Ari Smira, K. (1986). Cognitive and personality factors in the delay of gratification of hemodialysis patients. *Journal of Personality and Social Psychology, 51*, 357–364.

Rosenthal, R. (1991). *Meta-analytic procedures for social research.* Newbury Park, Calif.: Sage.

Rosenstock, I. M. (1966). Why people use health services. *Milbank Memorial Fund Quarterly, 44*, 94–124.

Rosser, W. W., Hutchison, B. G., McDowell, I., & Newell, C. (1992). Use of reminders to increase compliance with tetanus booster vaccination. *Canadian Medical Association Journal, 146*, 911–917.

Roter, D. L., Hall, J. A., Merisca, R., Nordstrom, B., Cretin, D., Svarstad, B. (1998). Effectiveness of interventions to improve patient compliance: A meta-analysis. *Medical Care, 36*, 1138–1161.

Roth, H. P. (1987). Current perspectives: Ten-year update on patient compliance research. *Patient Education and Counseling, 10*, 107–116.

Roth, H. P., & Caron, H. S. (1978). Accuracy of doctors' estimates and patients' statements on adherence to a drug regimen. *Clinical Pharmacology and Therapeutics, 23*, 361–370.

Rotter, J. B. (1966). Generalized expectancies for internal versus expectancies for external control of reinforcement. *Psychological Monographs, 80*, 609–615.

Rovelli, M., Palmeri, D., Vossler, E., Bartus, S., Hull, D., & Schweizer, R. (1989). Noncompliance in organ transplant recipients. *Transplantation Proceedings, 21*, 833–834.

Rozensky, R. H., & Bellack, A. S. (1976). Individual differences in self-reinforcement style and performance in self- and therapist-controlled weight reduction programs. *Behaviour Research & Therapy, 14*, 357–364.

Rudd, P. (1993). Partial compliance: Implications for clinical practice. *Journal of Cardiovascular Pharmacology, 22 (Suppl. A)*, S1–S5.

Rudd, P., Ahmed, S., Zachary, V., Barton, C., & Bonduelle, D. (1990). Improved compliance measures: Applications in an ambulatory hypertensive drug trial. *Clinical Pharmacology and Therapeutics, 48*, 676–685.

Rudman, L. A., Gonzales, M. H., & Borgida, E. (1999). Mishandling the gift of life: Noncompliance in renal transplant patients. *Journal of Applied Social Psychology, 29*, 834–851.

Rudy, T. E., Turk, D. C., Kubinski, J. A., & Hussien, S. Z. (1995). Differential treatment responses of TMD patients as a function of psychological characteristics. *Pain, 61,* 103–112.

Sackett, D. L., & Snow, J. C. (1979). The magnitude and measurement of compliance. In R. B. Haynes, D. W. Taylor, & D. L. Sackett (Eds.), *Compliance in Health Care.* Baltimore: Johns Hopkins University Press.

Safren, S. A., Otto, M. W., Worth, J. L., Salomon, E., Johnson, W., Mayer, K., & Boswell, S. (2001). Two strategies to increase adherence to HIV antiretroviral medication: Life-steps and medication monitoring. *Behaviour Research and Therapy, 39,* 1151–1162.

Sallis, J. F., Criqui, M. H., Kashani, I. A., Rupp, J. W., Calfas, K. J., Langer, R. D., Nader, P. R., & Ross, J., Jr. (1990). A program for health behavior change in a preventive cardiology center. *American Journal of Preventive Medicine, 6,* 43–50.

Schafer, L. C., Glasgow, R. E., & McCaul, K. D. (1982). Increasing the adherence of diabetic adolescents. *Journal of Behavioral Medicine, 5,* 353–362.

Schifter, D. B., & Ajzen, I. (1985). Intention, perceived control, and weight loss: An application of the theory of planned behavior. *Journal of Personality and Social Psychology, 49,* 843–851.

Schlenk, E. A., Dunbar-Jacob, J., Sereika, S., Starz, T., Okifuji, A., & Turk, D. (2000). Comparability of daily diaries and accelerometers in exercise adherence in fibromyalgia syndrome. *Measurement in Physical Education and Exercise Science, 4,* 133.

Schneider, M. S., Friend, R., Whitaker, P., & Wadhwa, N. K. (1991). Fluid noncompliance and symptomatology in end-stage renal disease: Cognitive and emotional variables. *Health Psychology, 10,* 209–215.

Schultheis, K., Peterson, L., & Selby, V. (1987). Preparation for stressful medical procedures and person treatment interactions. *Clinical Psychology Review, 7,* 329–352.

Sclar, D. A., Chin, A., Skaer, T. L., Okamoto, M. P., Nakahiro, R. K., & Gill, M. A. (1991). Effect of health education in promoting prescription refill compliance among patients with hypertension. *Clinical Therapeutics, 13,* 489–495.

Seibel, C. A., & Dowd, E. T. (1999). Reactance and therapeutic noncompliance. *Cognitive Therapy and Research, 23,* 373–379.

Sharma, A. K., Gupta, R., Tolani, S. L., Rathi, G. L., & Gupta, H. P. (2000). Evaluation of socioeconomic factors in noncompliance in renal transplantation. *Transplantation Proceedings, 32,* 1864.

Sheeran, P., Conner, M., & Norman, P. (2001). Can the theory of planned behavior explain patterns of health behavior change? *Health Psychology, 20,* 12–19.

Shepard, B. H., Hartwick, J., & Warshaw, P. R. (1988). The theory of reasoned action: A meta-analysis of past research with recommendations for modifications and future research. *Journal of Consumer Research, 15,* 325–343.

Sherbourne, C. D., Hays, R. D., Ordway, L., DiMatteo, M. R., & Kravitz, R. L. (1992). Antecedents of adherence to medical recommendations: Results from the medical outcomes study. *Journal of Behavioral Medicine, 15,* 447–468.

Sherman, J. M., Baumstein, S., & Hendeles, L. (2001). Intervention strategies for children poorly adherent with asthma medications; one center's experiences. *Clinical Pediatrics, 40,* 253–258.

Sherman, J., Hutson, A., Baumstein, S., & Hendeles, L. (2000). Telephoning the patient's pharmacy to assess adherence with asthma medications by measuring refill rate for prescriptions. *The Journal of Pediatrics, 136,* 532–536.

Shine, D., & McDonald, J. (1999). Limits of confidence in tracer compounds as a means of measuring patient compliance with medication. *Journal of Clinical Pharmacology, 39,* 1233–1241.

Simoni, J. M., Asarnow, J. R., Munford, P. R., Koprowski, C. M., Belin, T. R., & Salusky, I. B. (1997). Psychological distress and treatment adherence among children on dialysis. *Pediatric Nephrology, 11,* 604–606.

Smith, T. W. (1992). Hostility and health: Current status of a psychosomatic hypothesis. *Health Psychology, 11,* 139–150.

Smith, T. W., & Williams, P. G. (1992). Personality and health: Advantages and limitations of the Five-Factor Model. *Journal of Personality, 60,* 335–423.

Spector, S. L., Kinsman, R., Mawhinney, H., Siegel, S. C., Rachelefsky, G. S., Katz, R. M., & Rohr, A. S. (1986). Compliance of patients with asthma with an experimental aerosolized medication: Implications for controlled clinical trials. *The Journal of Allergy and Clinical Immunology, 77,* 65–70.

Stanton, A. L. (1987). Determinants of adherence to medical regimens by hypertensive patients. *Journal of Behavioral Medicine, 10,* 377–394.

Stein, J. A., Fox, S. A., Murata, P. J., & Morisky, D. E. (1992). Mammography usage and the health belief model. *Health Education Quarterly, 19,* 447–462.

Stephenson, J. (1999). Noncompliance may cause half of antihypertensive drug "failures." *The Journal of the American Medical Association, 282,* 313–314.

Stone, A. A., & Shiffman, S. (2002). Capturing momentary, self-report data: A proposal for reporting guidelines. *Annals of Behavioral Medicine, 24,* 236–243.

Stone, A. A., Turkkan, J., Jobe, J., Kurtzman, H., & Cain, V. (2000). *The science of self report.* Mahwah, N.J.: Lawrence Erlbaum Associates.

Stone, G. C. (1979). Patient compliance and the role of the expert. *Journal of Social Issues, 35,* 34–59.

Stoudemire, A., & Hales, R. E. (1995). Psychological factors affecting medical conditions and DSM-IV: An overview. In A. Stoudemire (Ed.), *Psychological factors affecting medical conditions.* Washington, D.C.: American Psychiatric Press.

Straka, R. J., Fish, J. T., Benson, S. R., & Suh, J. T. (1997). Patient self-reporting of compliance does not correspond with electronic monitoring: An evaluation using isosorbide dinitrate as a model drug. *Pharmacotherapy, 17,* 126–132.

Strecher, V. J., Champion, V. L., & Rosenstock, I. M. (1997). The health belief model and health behavior. In D. S. Gochman (Ed.), *Handbook of health behavior research I: Personal and social determinants* (pp. 71–91). New York: Plenum Press.

Strickland, B. R. (1978). Internal-external expectancies and health-related behaviors. *Journal of Consulting and Clinical Psychology, 46,* 1192–1211.

Stuart, R. B. (1967). Behavioural control of overeating. *Behavioural Research and Therapy, 5,* 357–365.

Suls, J., & Sanders, G. S. (1989). Why do some behavioral styles place people at coronary risk? In A. W. Siegman & T. M. Dembroski (Eds.), *In search of coronary-prone behavior: Beyond type A* (pp. 1–20). Hillsdale, N.J.: Lawrence Erlbaum Associates.

Swain, M. A., & Steckel, S. B. (1981). Influencing adherence among hypertensives. *Research in Nursing and Health, 4,* 213–222.

Swanson, M., Hull, D., Bartus, S., & Schweizer, R. (1992). Economic impact of noncompliance in kidney transplant recipients. *Transplantation Proceedings, 24,* 2722.

Taylor, C. B., Houston-Miller, N., Killen, J. D., DeBusk, R. F. (1990). Smoking cessation after acute myocardial infarction: Effects of a nurse-managed intervention. *Annals of Internal Medicine, 113,* 118–123.

Taylor, D. W. (1979). A test of the health belief model in hypertension. In R. B. Haynes, D. W. Taylor, & D. L. Sackett (Eds.), *Compliance in health care* (pp. 103–109). Baltimore, Md.: John Hopkins University Press.

Taylor, S. E. (1979). Hospital patient behavior: Reactance, helplessness, or control? *Journal of Social Issues, 35,* 156–184.

Taylor, S. E. (1983). Adjustment to threatening events: A theory of cognitive adaptation. *American Psychologist, 41,* 1161–1173.

Taylor, S. E., Helgeson, V. S., Reed, G. M., & Skokan, L. A. (1991). Self-generated feelings of control and adjustment to physical illness. *Journal of Social Issues, 47,* 91–109.

Telch, C. F., Agras, W. S., Rossiter, E. M., Wilfley, D., & Kenardy, J. (1990). Group cognitive-behavioral treatment for the non-purging bulimic: An initial evaluation. *Journal of Consulting and Clinical Psychology, 58,* 629–635.

Thom, D. H., & Stanford Trust Study Physicians (2001). Physician behaviors that predict patient trust. *The Journal of Family Practice, 50,* 323–328.

Thompson, C. J., Cummings, F., Chalmers, J., & Newton, R. W. (1995). Abnormal insulin treatment behaviour: A major cause of ketoacidosis in the young adult. *Diabetic Medicine, 12,* 429–432.

Thomsett, M., Shield, G., Batch, J., & Cotterill, A. (1999). How well are we doing? Metabolic control in patients with diabetes. *Journal of Paediatrics and Child Health, 35,* 479–482.

Trostle, J. A. (1997). The history and meaning of patient compliance as an ideology. In D. S. Gochman (Ed.), *Handbook of health behavior research II: Provider determinants* (pp. 109–124). New York: Plenum Press.

Turk, D. C., & Kerns, R. D. (1985). The family in health and illness. In D. C. Turk & R. D. Kerns (Eds.), *Health, Illness, and Families: A Life-Span Perspective.* (pp. 1–22). New York: Wiley.

Turk, D. C., Okifuji, A., Sinclair, J. D., & Starz, T. W. (1998). Differential responses by psychosocial subgroups of fibromyalgia syndrome patients to an interdisciplinary treatment. *Arthritis Care, 11,* 307–404.

Turk, D. C., & Meichenbaum, D. (1991). Adherence to self-care regimens: The patient's persepective. In J. J. Sweet, R. H. Rozensky, & S. M. Tovian (Eds.), *Handbook of clinical psychology in medical settings* (pp. 249–266). New York: Plenum Press.

Urquhart, J., & Chevalley, C. (1988). Impact of unrecognized dosing errors on the cost and effectiveness of pharmaceuticals. *Drug Information Journal, 22,* 363–378.

Van der Bij, A. K., Laurant, M. G., & Wensing, M. (2002). Effectiveness of physical activity interventions for older adults: A review. *American Journal of Preventive Medicine, 22,* 120–133.

Van der Meer, J. T., van Wijk, W., Thompson, J., Valkenburg, H. A., & Michel, M. F. (1992). Awareness of need and actual use of prophylaxis: Lack of patient compliance in the prevention of bacterial endocarditis. *The Journal of Antimicrobial Chemotherapy, 29,* 187–194.

Van Es, S. M., Nagelkerke, A. F., Colland, V. T., Scholten, R. J., & Bouter, L. M. (2001). An intervention programme using the ASE-model aimed at enhancing adherence in adolescents with asthma. *Patient Education Counseling, 44,* 193–203.

Wallston, K. A. (1992). Hocus-pocus, the focus isn't strictly on locus: Rotter's social learning theory modified for health. *Cognitive Therapy and Research, 16,* 183–199.

Wallston, K. A., & Wallston, B. S. (1982). Who is responsible for your health? The construct of health locus of control. In G. Sanders & J. Suls (Eds.), *Social psychology of health and illness* (pp. 65–95). Hillsdale, N.J.: Lawrence Erlbaum Associates.

Wallston, K. A., Wallston, B. S., & DeVellis, R. (1978). Development of the multidimensional health locus of control (MHLC) scales. *Health Education Monographs, 6,* 160–170.

Waterhouse, D. M., Calzone, K. A., Mele, C., & Brenner, D. E. (1993). Adherence to oral tamoxifen: A comparison of patient self-report, pill counts, and microelectronic monitoring. *Journal of Clinical Oncology, 11,* 1189–1197.

Webb, P. A. (1980). Effectiveness of patient education and psychosocial counseling in promoting compliance and control among hypertensive patients. *The Journal of Family Practice, 10*, 1047–1055.

Weinberger, M., Tierney, W. M., Booher, P., & Katz, B. P. (1991). The impact of increased contact on psychosocial outcomes in patients with osteoarthritis: A randomized, controlled trial. *Journal of Rheumatology, 18*, 849–854.

Wiebe, D. J., Alderfer, M. A., Palmer, S. C., Linday, R., & Jarrett, L. (1994). Behavioral self-regulation in adolescents with type I diabetes: Negative affectivity and blood glucose symptom perception. *Journal of Consulting and Clinical Psychology, 62*, 1204–1212.

Wiebe, J. S., & Christensen, A. J. (1996). Patient adherence in chronic illness: Personality and coping in context. *Journal of Personality, 64*, 815–835.

Wiebe, J. S., & Christensen, A. J. (1997). Conscientiousness, health beliefs, and patient adherence in renal dialysis. *Annals of Behavioral Medicine, 19*, 30–35.

Weingarten, M. A., & Cannon, B. S. (1988). Age as a major factor affecting adherence to medication for hypertension in a general practice population. *Family Practice, 5*, 294–296.

Williams, R. L., Maiman, L. A., Broadbent, D. N., Kotok, D., Lawrence, R. A., Longfield, L. A., Mangold, A. H., Mayer, S. J., Powell, K. R., Sayre, J. W., et al. (1986). Educational strategies to improve compliance with an antibiotic regimen. *American Journal of Diseases of Children, 140*, 216–220.

Williams, G. C., Rodin, G. C., Ryan, R. M., Grolnick, W. S., & Deci, E. L. (1998). Autonomous regulation and long-term medication adherence in adult outpatients. *Health Psychology, 17*, 269–276.

Wills, T. A. & Filer, M. (2001). Social networks and social support. In A. Baum, T. Revenson, & J. Singer (Eds.), *Handbook of Health Psychology* (pp. 209–234). Mahaw, N.J.: Lawrence Erlbaum Associates.

Wing, A. J. (1984). Choosing a dialysis therapy: Narrative summary of a panel discussion. *American Journal of Kidney Disease, IV*, 256–259.

Wing, R. A. (2002). Behavioral weight control. In T. Wadden & A. Stunkard (Eds.), *Handbook of Obesity Treatment* (pp. 301–316). New York: Gulford Press.

Wing, R. A, Epstein, L. H., Nowalk, M. P., Scott, N., Koeske, R., & Hagg, S. (1986). Does self-monitoring of blood glucose levels improve dietary compliance for obese patients with type II diabetes? *American Journal of Medicine, 81*, 830–836.

Wittenberg, S. H., Blanchard, E. B., Suls, J., Tennen, H., McCoy, G., & McGoldrick, M. D. (1983). Perceptions of control and causality as predictors of compliance and coping in hemodialysis. *Basic and Applied Social Psychology, 4*, 319–336.

Wolcott, D. L., Maida, C. A., Diamond, R., & Nissenson, A. R. (1986). Treatment compliance in end-stage renal disease patients on dialysis. *American Journal of Nephrology, 6*, 329–338.

Wysocki, T., Green, L., & Huxtable, K. (1989). Blood glucose monitoring by diabetic adolescents: compliance and metabolic control. *Health Psychology,*
8, 267–284.

Wysocki, T., Harris, M. A., Greco, P., Bubb, J., Danda, C. E., Harvey, L. M.,
McDonell, K., Taylor, A., & White, N. H. (2000). Randomized, controlled trial of behavior therapy for families of adolescents with insulin-
dependent diabetes mellitus. *Journal of Pediatric Psychology, 25,* 23–33.

Zahr, L. K., Yazigi, A, & Armenian, H. (1989). The effect of education and written material on compliance of pediatric clients. *International Journal of*
Nursing Studies, 26, 213–220.

Zyzanski, S. J., Stange, K. C., Langa, D., & Flocke, S. A. (1998). Trade-offs in
high-volume primary care practice. *The Journal of Family Practice, 46,*
397–402.

Credits

Figure 1.2 (page 16). Printed with permission, AARDEX Ltd., 2002.

Figure 4.3 (page 72). From Christensen et al. (1994), Patient adherence and adjustment in renal dialysis: A person by treatment interactional approach. *Journal of Behavioral Medicine, 17,* 549–566. Reprinted with permission, Kluwer Academic/Plenum Publishers.

Figure 4.4 (page 75). From Christensen (2000), Patient X treatment context interaction in chronic disease: A conceptual framework for the study of patient adherence. *Psychosomatic Medicine, 62,* 435–443. Reprinted with permission, Lippincott, Williams, & Wilkins.

Figure 4.5 (page 79). From Christensen et al. (1997), Monitoring attentional style and medical regimen adherence. *Health Psychology, 16,* 256–262. Copyright 1997 by the American Psychological Association. Reprinted with permission.

Table 5.2 (page 86). From Christensen et al. (2002), Effect of a behavioral self-regulation intervention on patient adherence in hemodialysis. *Health Psychology, 21,* 393–397. Copyright 2002 by the American Psychological Association. Reprinted with permission.

Figure 5.1 (page 87). From Christensen et al. (2002), Effect of behavioral self-regulation intervention on patient adherence in hemodialysis. *Health Psychology, 21,* 393–397. Copyright 2002 by the American Psychological Association. Reprinted with permission.

Index